To —
To a fellow
aviator)
Grant

A GOOD STICK

AN AIRLINE CAPTAIN LIVES THE HISTORY OF 20TH CENTURY COMMERCIAL AVIATION

BY

JERRY SORLUCCO

authorHOUSE™

1663 LIBERTY DRIVE, SUITE 200
BLOOMINGTON, INDIANA 47403
(800) 839-8640
WWW.AUTHORHOUSE.COM

First published by AuthorHouse 08/09/05

ISBN: 1-4208-4845-3 (e)
ISBN: 1-4208-4843-7 (sc)
ISBN: 1-4208-4844-5 (dj)

Library of Congress Control Number: 2005903446

Printed in the United States of America
Bloomington, Indiana

This book is printed on acid-free paper.

In memory of my parents, Marie and Jerry Sorlucco, who gave me life, love and confidence.

And for the pathfinders in the golden age of aviation, who took an immigrant's son from Brooklyn and taught him how to fly, both in body and soul.

Acknowledgements

I first met Tim McCarthy when he was the editor of *The Courier,* a weekly newspaper in Littleton, New Hampshire. As a political activist I'd submit letters to the editor and op-eds that more likely than not would find their way into the paper. I'm a progressive Democrat in a tightly conservative town so Tim would get letters fired back, and he'd publish those as well. Sometimes it got pretty lively.

The paper fired Tim shortly after I decided to run for the New Hampshire state Senate. No reason was given, but everyone knew it was because his editorials were just a little too liberal for the conservative and relatively new owners. I offered Tim an ill-paying job as my campaign writer and manager; he came on board and we've been dear friends and colleagues ever since.

During the campaigns—there were two—we spent countless hours driving around the North Country. With his prodding, I'd tell him stories about my long airline career and my early days in aviation. When the campaign was over, Tim encouraged me to write a memoir, suggesting that if he enjoyed the stories so would others. If the book shines it is because he has worked hand-in-hand with me as a mentor and collaborating editor—he's a tough teacher.

We developed a great team that includes my very special and gifted wife Sue and Olivia Garfield. Olivia and her husband Doug were the former owners of *The Courier* and had hired Tim years before as editor. Olivia sold her share in the paper after Doug died. She is a great editor in her own right, with a fantastic eye for catching grammatical errors. Sue did the photographic restorations and related artwork—not a simple task because some of the pictures are over half a century old.

To the team, my deepest thanks.

Final Flight to Frankfurt

I have often wondered what it must have been like, say, for those who survived the blast in the Pan American Flight 103 that exploded 31,000 feet over Lockerbie, Scotland in 1988. They found the captain, the first officer and a flight attendant still in the cockpit, which was pretty much intact. Forensic evidence showed that some of the passengers and crew were conscious at least some of the way down. What was it like for those people in those last seconds of consciousness after they were blown free into a blaze of stars, before their long descent into death?

My career didn't end in disaster, or in wreckage of any kind, but even in the days before the so-called war on terror airline crews were well aware that something similar could happen on almost any flight. Most of us did not dwell on it. Still, it occurs to me now that the downing of Pan Am 103, along with a whole history of airline disasters, resonated through my final flight as a commercial airline captain with a far lesser though no less certain finality. After nearly forty years of total command and the responsibility for thousands upon thousands of people, I was about to be grounded. Federal regulations were forcing me to retire at age sixty. Yet even now, years into retirement, I sometimes feel that I am still strapped in my cockpit.

That final flight left Boston's Logan Airport on July 7, 1997, and returned from Frankfurt, Germany July 9, one day before my sixtieth birthday. My career spanned much of the history of commercial aviation in the last century. After years of flying marginal aircraft in the toughest regional airline environment in the world, I was being forced out of the best duty of my career—flying the North Atlantic route for US Airways. I was a highly respected number one on our seniority list and probably the most senior captain on Earth. That is pretty heady stuff.

Throughout my career, I ran a highly professional flight deck and crew. In my thirty-five years as a captain, I never once raised my voice. Pros don't do that. As a professional, I was tough-minded and in control, yet I can be easily touched emotionally at times. Maybe that's part of my Italian heritage, I don't know. But I did know that the retirement flight would include a salute to a departing comrade and I would have preferred simply to go home quietly. A tearful captain isn't the John Wayne image I wanted to leave behind. I truly considered calling in sick. Now I'm glad that I didn't.

There have been some wild last trips—antics such as low altitude flybys of your neighborhood. "What the hell," some pilots might say, "they can't fire me now." But that was not my style. This final flight to Frankfurt was briefed and planned just like any other.

Flight planning a North Atlantic crossing is interesting. Once over the ocean, it is like being on it. You are in international airspace. No one owns or controls it. There are coastal fixed airways as there are over land, but over the North Atlantic Tracks (NAT) they change twice a day—twice a day because ninety-nine percent of the traffic goes east, North America to Europe, in the evening East Coast time and returns in the morning western European time, arriving in the United States in the afternoon.

So, to plan a flight you take the published NAT tracks and plot a primary requested track and two adjacent tracks by scrupulously entering latitude and longitudes for the route on a planning chart. The tracks are required to be sixty nautical miles apart. An error entered into the flight management computer can and has put aircraft into someone else's airspace. To avoid these errors, flight planning is ritualized. All entries are spoken aloud and crosschecked by two pilots at every step. The US Airways system was widely accepted and imitated as the industry standard.

International crew briefings are scheduled for an hour and a half before flight time. As was my habit, I was always early (I once showed up by mistake a day ahead of time). All the dispatchers, who are responsible for releasing the airline's international flights, waited for me to call. I knew them all and they all knew that I had better weather and aircraft status briefings than anybody. I also religiously briefed the flight attendants on security considerations, time en route and expected turbulence. That night I expected a smooth trip and on-time arrival. The briefing enabled them to plan cabin service, along with their other duties. I treated them with respect and as a team and they always responded in spades.

****

Flight 816 was scheduled to leave Logan at 7:10 p.m. and arrive in Frankfurt seven hours and twenty minutes later at 8:30 a.m. local time. The weather was good over the whole route and the aircraft full, or close to full.

The only aircraft US Airways flew overseas at that time was the Boeing 767-200ER. "ER" stands for extended range. The 76, as we called it, is powered by two General Electric CF6-80C2 engines rated at 60,000 pounds of thrust each, which equates to 60,000 horsepower at about 280 knots. A man standing beside one of those engines is dwarfed. With a wingspan of a little over 156 feet, length of 155 feet, tail height of 52 feet, and a maximum takeoff weight of 351,000 pounds, the 76 is an impressive aircraft. There are also five bathrooms, two galleys, and eleven crewmembers to accommodate up to 210 passengers.

On an international flight, the crew includes the captain, first officer and international relief officer (IRO). There is a flight attendant in charge, one assigned as purser and a LODO, one who speaks the languages of destination and origin. The IRO is a pilot, usually junior, required for flights over eight hours. That allows one of the two operating pilots to leave the flight deck for a nap, or simply to take a break.

There are four seats on the flight deck. The captain is up front left, the first officer on the right. Although the 76 was the first large aircraft designed without a flight engineer, there is a station

3

provided for one. The fourth seat is a fold down behind the captain. Jump seat riders are usually authorized pilots or Federal Aviation Administration officials, but flight attendants also use the seat to take a break.

On that last flight from Logan, I got permission for my former colleague Dave Phipps to use the jump seat. One of the retirement flight perks is that the airline offers complimentary seats to your family and friends. My wife Sue also got a free ride on Flight 816. A few years junior to me, Dave had retired several years earlier because of back problems. We did a lot of union work together during the early years and have remained friends ever since. A slim man with craggy good looks and a rakish mustache, Dave is a walking dichotomy. Extremely conservative politically, he was at the same time a highly effective union representative for most of his flying career. He is also one of the funniest people I have ever known. Through the years we have had plenty of laughs as well as arguments and more than a few beers.

That night, Dave boarded the airplane with me. Sue came on later with the other passengers. I always made it a point to speak to the chief agent at the gate. This went a long way toward avoiding delays and, in later years, helped to deal with security concerns. As I remember, we were on time that night and everything was normal--except, maybe, for me. Sixty is a young age to force a professional person from work. I had fought the age 60 rule for years and was a founder and vice president of the Professional Pilots Federation. The PPF's sole mission was to remove or increase the arbitrary age limit imposed by the Federal Aviation Administration. As we began that final flight from Logan, those years weighed upon me, a bit of the bitter, perhaps, in that bittersweet experience.

From the time you enter the cockpit, there is a routine. You are checking things all along the way. Of course, being the captain is great. Once on board, you have more authority than just about anyone on Earth. It is all based upon maritime law, which leaves the captain totally in charge. The flip side is that you are responsible. Someone else messing up doesn't change that. The drill is that you should have caught the screw-up; you should have double checked.

Usually, the IRO—for this flight a pilot named Tom Tydmen— would do the "walk around." This is a physical inspection of the outside of the aircraft, checking for damage, tire and brake wear, leaks, closed hatches, and more. Occasionally, I would do the walk around myself. The 76 is such a beautiful aircraft. I enjoyed looking at it. And the walk around gave me a chance to smooze with the mechanics and ground crew.

Once in the seat, things get even more serious. First, the aircraft has to be positioned on the Earth's surface. The precise longitude and latitude of the airport gate are entered into the Inertia Reference Systems. There are two. The technology came from the space program, as did our Honeywell flight management systems, also two.

Then the captain and the first officer perform other preflight procedures, including a cockpit switch position scan and the Normal Procedures Cockpit Checklist. There are also Emergency Check Lists and a book full of procedures.

After the aircraft's position is fixed in the Inertia Reference Systems, the next step is to enter the entire flight plan, in this case Boston (BOS) to Frankfurt (FRA), into the flight management systems by way of the Control Display Units. It is quite a lengthy procedure, always cross read by two pilots.

In the cockpit of a big airplane you are sitting high off the ground. You can't see any other part of the ship, unless you crane your neck with your nose up against the side window, which gives you a limited view of a wing tip. You communicate with the ground crew by intercom through the mechanic out in front wearing a headset. It is a dangerous business. Crossed signals have caused people to be hurt or killed as the aircraft is pushed back and the engines started prior to taxi.

The 76 has a self-contained auxiliary power unit—a fairly large turbine engine that supplies electrical power, air-conditioning, and the air pressure required to start the engines. A jet engine is like an enormous vacuum cleaner sucking air in the front and igniting it with fuel, which generates the thrust that roars out the back. Both ends are dangerous. People have been sucked in the front, not a pleasant prospect, to say the least.

Good procedures, standard routine: I'd done it tens of thousands of times, but always with extreme diligence and concentration. An airline pilot axiom says you are only as good as your last landing.

That degree of concentration is a strain on marriage and other relationships. But if you are sitting in the cockpit worried about a wife at home, a sick child, or anything else you can think of, you're not worth a damn. The shrinks call it compartmentalizing. Some guys dealt with it well. Others never did. For them, their last flight was a relief. I never felt that way, but now, retired for over five years, I realize more what a strain it was between Sue and me. And I am, after all, also a divorce statistic. Everything has a price. And yet, that shared responsibility with a flight crew led to some of closest relationships I have ever had.

Fear was another factor and it had similar results. When I started to fly, I experienced fear at different times and overcame it with knowledge and the need to continue flying. Some pilots never do overcome it, which makes for a tortured career. They do the job with dread instead of joy. On the other hand, anyone who sits at the front of a 350,000-pound aluminum missile loaded with 120,000 pounds of jet fuel and doesn't think it might be a bit dangerous, you'd really have to worry about.

****

Takeoff that night was on runway 22L with a Logan One Departure, which outlines the initial climb out procedures. The runway is 10,005 feet long. The departure has an immediate left turn to a heading of 140 degrees, usually at a low level so as to pass under arriving aircraft. That can be challenging, because once it's unleashed all that power wants to take you to the moon, not level off at 1,000 or 2,000 feet.

On long-range flights, you "step climb," or climb at intervals, as fuel is burned and weight reduced. Ocean crossings are usually between 32,000 and 38,000 feet. (Altitudes above 18,000 feet are expressed as Flight Levels, such as FL32, FL38, and so on. FLs are calibrated from a standard barometric pressure of 29.92, so they are not the exact altitude above the surface, which changes with the local barometer reading.)

At those high altitudes, the night sky over the North Atlantic is so beautiful that I never tired of looking at it. Because you are above any haze and free of refracted light, it is like being in a planetarium.

As a kid, I loved going to the Hayden Planetarium next door to the Museum of Natural History in Manhattan. I often thought that sitting up front in a 76 was a long way to climb for a kid from Brooklyn.

Particularly during the winter months the aurora borealis, better known as the Northern Lights, are spectacular. Meteors are a dime a dozen and the constellations sparkle like diamonds. One night we had it all: The comet Hale-Bopp was clearly visible, tail and all; there was a brilliant moon and the aurora borealis glowed like the northern dawn its name implies. What a magnificent spectacle! That night I made sure all the flight attendants got up to the cockpit to see it.

The more earthly dawn comes on like an express train, first as a glow and then the sun simply pops up. Actually, with a timed descent, you could have two sunrises because of the Earth's curvature. It was all great fun, even awe-inspiring.

Your first contact after landfall heading east is with Shannon, Ireland. You identify yourself and give Shannon the waypoint you are over and your altitude (FL370). From that point, you leave the North Atlantic Tracks system and enter a radar environment.

The universal air traffic control language is English, although a few countries allow the native language to be spoken as well. Ironically, I always found the Brits harder to understand than the Germans. The French could be difficult to understand as well, but whatever their nationality they were all extremely professional and great to work with.

On Tuesday, July 8, 1997, US Airways 816 touched down on runway 25R, Frankfurt/Main Airport, on time at about 8:10 local time on a nice sunny morning. The landing was smooth (a "grease job," as pilots like to call it).

****

US Airways parking at the Frankfurt airport is at remote gates quite far from the terminal. Buses take the passengers in and a separate bus is provided for the crew. We now had a scheduled layover of about twenty-six hours in nearby Wiesbaden.

The ride from the airport to the Holiday Inn Crown Plaza in downtown Wiesbaden takes about half an hour. Wiesbaden is noted for its natural hot spring baths around which developed an art culture. There is a world-renowned opera house, a gambling casino and hundreds of shops and restaurants. It was also one of the few cities along the Rhine River to escape Allied bombing during World War II. Legend has it that Winston Churchill, the British prime minister during the war, had a mistress there. For whatever reason, Wiesbaden is one of the few places in postwar Germany that has beautiful original structures, including a fantastic brick cathedral on a square just a few blocks from the hotel.

US Airways had three crews daily overnight at the Crown Plaza (flights from Boston, Pittsburgh and Charlotte, North Carolina). Thirty-three rooms a night is a pretty good contract for any hotel and on the whole the Crown Plaza treated us well. But often housekeeping wouldn't have our rooms ready because of the short turnover time between crews. The wait usually wasn't long, but crews were tired and ended up camped all over the lobby.

We all had our own RON (remain overnight) routine. If the rooms weren't ready, some guys would change in the john and go run. I went to the corner bakery that made wonderful breads and pastries. It also offered assorted prepared sandwiches that were great. Next stop was the newspaper/smoke shop on the other corner. It had an extensive selection of German beer and wine. By the time I got back to the hotel, my room was usually ready and up I'd go to enjoy my treats and usually read a book. I always had one with me.

On the layovers, you had to plan your sleep time for two days within the twenty-six hours. If you slept too much when you got in, you'd be staring at the ceiling for hours before the trip out. I would be asleep within an hour, having set an alarm for three hours later. That would be about 1 p.m. The rooms had heavy window drapes to keep the light out. Traditional German feather comforters covered the bed. Only trouble was, the hotel was old and the air-conditioning insufficient. During the summer months, my choice was usually open windows and noise.

When I awoke, I would dress in exercise clothes and head for the hotel restaurant for some gutsy German coffee and a pastry, and then either use the hotel gym or, weather permitting, go for a jog or fast walk in the splendid park system that is an integral part of the city. Sometimes a crewmember would join me.

The pro who took care of the hotel pool, gym and sauna was a character. A lifelong bachelor, he vacationed every year in Cuba, a favorite German destination. He said he had a young girlfriend in Havana whom he might marry and bring back to Germany, but I don't think he was serious about it. He hit on some of the flight attendants, but was manageable and not a problem.

The park jog or walk that I liked was about three miles round-trip. From next to the opera house, the park opened into a large area that included an amphitheater and a kiosk selling beer, wine and an assortment of sausages. On the opposite side, a small pond featured paddleboats you could rent to pump your way through a dense flock of swans. An orchestra played American big band music on summer Saturdays. What a rush from the past it was to hear Glen Miller in Wiesbaden the first Saturday I jogged by. From there, I followed a wooded path for about a mile and a half along the stream that feeds the pond. Then there was a short climb up a steep hill to an old hotel that – guess what? – served beer at an outside seating area with a marvelous view.

A second, more ambitious jog went down to the Rhine and along the river. Of course there were those ubiquitous pubs to tempt a thirsty jogger on that route, too. Germans are seldom far from their beer. Tour boats would take you past the river's famous castles and vineyards. If you were willing to sacrifice a little sleep on a short layover, a river tour was a pleasant way to spend an afternoon.

All told, Wiesbaden is a great small city. It has a population of about 50,000. With its parks, its pedestrian streets closed to automobiles, its plethora of restaurants and pubs with outside seating, it is a people oriented place. American planners interested in walk able towns could learn a lot there.

Exercise and a shower would usually shake off some of the jet lag. Then I would go to meet any crewmembers who showed up, either in the hotel lobby or around the corner at Inga's pub. When we started staying in Wiesbaden, a grouchy old guy who hated Americans owned the pub. Then, Lord be praised, Inga bought the place and life was good. Inga had a stimulating body and she loved the flight crews. Needless to say, the crews loved her right back. She carried all the top German beers, each served in its own special glass.

9

Unfortunately, she didn't serve meals, so the big decision was where to go from there. And a tough decision it was, given Wiesbaden's many good restaurants.

Right next door to Inga's was a place with an extensive menu. Its specialty was rotary broiled chicken. Usually, there were a dozen or more birds turning at a time. They did a big take-out business and served delicious half-chicken meals.

An earlier choice was a truly neighborhood pub called Shots. Shots offered a limited menu built around schnitzel. Schnitzel, of course, is a breaded cutlet, either veal or pork. Shots prepared schnitzel in a half dozen ways, all of them gratifying to almost anyone's appetite. The owner was a young man from the former East Germany. He called the place "Shots" because after every meal he served a round of firewater that would take the skin off your tongue. I don't know if the stuff even had a name.

All this may give you some idea of why Wiesbaden was a great place to layover for the night, a far cry from my early flying days. But, whether in a cheap motel or first class hotel, I've spent a good part of my life on the road. It was a wonderful career but, as I've said, everything has its price. The guys and gals who did it well lived in the moment. They didn't put life on hold until they got home. We had guys who would take snacks from the aircraft, rather than spend money on a meal, then never venture from their hotel room. I chose to live every day to the fullest. It was a decision I never regretted.

Mind you, I'd call home on every trip, much to the delight of the telephone company. But it was worth every penny to stay in touch. It is a terrible thing that so many in our society suffer such guilt because of the demands our culture puts on marriage and family at the expense of self. I was not immune to this conflict, although on the whole I think I handled it well.

Anyway, I still spent a lot time alone. It went with the job. But, an avid reader since childhood, I always had a book along for company.

****

I have photographs of our crew, along with Sue and Dave Phipps, sitting in front of Inga's on that July afternoon after we landed in

Frankfurt. As I look at our group relaxing on red plastic chairs around small, white tables, I am grateful for my years as an airline pilot. It was the golden age of aviation. By comparison, it breaks my heart to see what today's pilots are enduring. But more of that later.

It's not that we had a free ride. We had to fight like hell for everything we got. But we gave back. In the fifty years after World War II, we created an air transportation system that brought the world together. Pilots were paid well because the tremendous skill and responsibility their job required demanded it. At the same time, well-managed airlines were able to capitalize billions of dollars of jet age equipment and make a profit free of cutthroat competition. That is no longer the case.

As we sat at Inga's in 1997, the airline industry was troubled and uncertain, but there was optimism. Under President Bill Clinton, the economy was flying high and the world was probably as close to being at peace as it ever will be. Now, after the terrorist attacks on New York and Washington in 2001 and two years under George W. Bush, we are in what is most likely the deepest recession since the Great Depression and optimism is hard to come by.

But God is good and the future was way over the horizon during that last layover in Wiesbaden. The crew made a decision. It was to be German food at a restaurant we had recently discovered about a half-mile away.

Dining throughout Europe, and certainly in Wiesbaden, is not a rushed affair. Waiters are in no hurry to take your order and they don't hover over you in an effort to turn the table over to new customers. To the uninitiated, that could seem like poor service, but it isn't. It is simply showing respect for the dining experience. Our dinner party that night was very much in the leisurely tradition.

Larry, the first officer, proposed the first toast. Others followed. Larry is tall and slim and extremely articulate, which was a blessing the next day on the last flight home, because he did all the announcements. Like Dave, Larry wears a mustache, although not with the panache Dave has cultivated. Dave's humor did not fail him that night. Once again he managed to tickle our funny bones and touch our hearts.

With Sue sitting beside me, I knew that my future was going to be just fine. Life would merely enter a new and uncharted phase. Much to my surprise, I didn't get emotional and I had a marvelous time.

When we left the restaurant, I was absolutely sated with good feelings. What a difficult experience to describe! My mind ran the gambit, from a five-year-old reading about aviation and World War II, to the emerging 21st century. I guess one of my regrets is that I did not get to fly into the millennium. Anyway, it was all a far cry from an early memory of flying a kite with my father on the roof of 4812-7th Avenue in Brooklyn. Although I did not know it at the time, my father was truly one of my heroes.

Brooklyn Boyhood

It all started in Brooklyn, New York.

My mother, Marie, was born in Bennevento, Italy on February 25, 1913 to Theresa and Philamino Manginello. Bennevento is inland from Naples. My grandfather and mother both described the family as farmers. Grandfather used to beguile me as a young child with tales of sleeping outdoors and having to guard against snakes that he assured me could and did wrap around the careless and strangle them to death. I still don't like snakes very much!

Mother didn't see her father until she was seven years old at the Ellis Island immigration facility in New York Harbor. Grandfather had immigrated to America shortly after her birth to avoid being conscripted into the Italian army at the outbreak of World War I. He had a sister living in Hackensack, New Jersey, who sponsored him. He found work as a lamplighter in Brooklyn. Gas lamps still provided the street lighting then and they had to be lit, turned off and serviced. He sent money home regularly and after the war ended was able to send for his family. Mother spoke of the boat ride traveling steerage and the kind people who took a shine to her and gave her food.

This was the time of the great American melting pot. New York City's population was 1,515,301 in 1890, 3,437,202 in 1900, 4,766,883 in 1910 and, when Mother's boat landed in 1920, it was 5,620,048. In 1940, three years after I came along, it was 7,454,995.

13

The immigrants were mostly from Ireland and Italy, but there were plenty of Germans and Norwegians as well. Interestingly, after the 1940 census, the population went down due to the great post World War II move to suburbia. By 2000, it had increased again to 8,008,278.

The Manginellos settled in on Reeve's Place, a side street on the west side of Prospect Park in Brooklyn. Mother went to public school, PS-130. Although she didn't speak a word of English, a teacher took her under her wing and gave mother both her new language and a new name, Marie. Her baptismal name was Maria-Conchetta, but the teacher thought Marie was more American. I went to PS-130 and had that same teacher in the eighth grade. You can't say that wonderful woman didn't earn her money!

When Mother was thirteen, twin baby brothers were born into the family. One was Ralph; the other died an infant. Not many years later my grandmother, Theresa, died suddenly of what they thought was a stroke. No one ever really knew. So my mother became a teenage mother to her brother. She managed to graduate from the eighth grade before she had to go to work and care for my uncle Ralph. I know she worked at the Pilgrim Laundry and did so again when I was a child and we needed the money. My grandfather by then had found a job at a Jewish cemetery in Flatbush as a gravedigger, stone setter, or whatever else had to be done. It was hard work that he did into his seventies and he loved it. His buddies gave him the name Patsy; Philamino just didn't cut the mustard.

Around the time, my grandmother Theresa died and Mother met my father to be, Gernaro Sorlucco, "Jerry." Father was the oldest son of an Italian immigrant family that lived at 402-4th. Avenue in a tough neighborhood. He was born in Brooklyn, followed by two brothers and five sisters. My grandfather Basel was deported back to Naples as an illegal immigrant, leaving my grandmother Mary and the children behind. He was never seen again.

Like my mother, Father had also managed to get through the eighth grade, but as the eldest in his family he had to work as many jobs as you could after that.

The story goes that Mother and Father met at a concert in Prospect Park. Both had heavy family responsibilities and no marriage ensued for a too long a time to suit Mother. It's said there was another suitor in the running but, much to that man's regret, I'm sure, Father grew able to support his own family and he married my mother.

They set up home on 17th Street off 7th Avenue, also off Prospect Park. Having had some involvement in town planning, I now realize the genius of those city planners who pushed through the New York City park system. In Brooklyn, there is Prospect Park and in Manhattan Central Park. There are smaller parks such as Sunset Park and Ocean Parkway, a main road with a bridle path on one side and a walking, bicycle path on the other, that runs right down the middle of Brooklyn to the ocean at Coney Island. Unfortunately, the bridle path is long gone and the beautiful homes have given way to high rise apartment buildings.

Brooklyn also has one of the largest cemeteries in the world, Greenwood Cemetery. Mother, Father and most of my ancestors are buried there.

I came along on July 10, 1937. Some of my earliest memories are of 17th Street, Uncle Ralph scolding me about potty training, riding on my father's shoulders and meals at Grandmother Sorlucco's. I also remember a corner candy store where for a penny you could look through a viewer, turn a wheel and see cards flip over to make a movie.

Holiday meals at Grandmother's were always an event. There was little money but boy the food was good. Always there'd be homemade ravioli. I'd help crimp the sides to lock in the regatta cheese and then carry them over to the next room to be put on sheet over a bed to dry. The seats around the table were always full and somehow a bottle of wine always appeared.

All I knew of Mother's mother was what Mother told me. Pictures of her show that she was also a big woman dressed in black. Both women had big hearts that came through to me by my parents. Truth is, I was spoiled rotten and loved it. When I was five or six years old, Mother had a miscarriage that threatened her life, so I remained an only child.

In the years just before World War II, FDR's programs to lift the country out of the depression were helping, but times were still damn tough. I remember one Christmas when father lucked out because of a snowstorm. The city hired men to shovel snow and he was able to make a few extra bucks for the holiday. Our Christmas tree didn't arrive until fairly late Christmas Eve; he got one that was left over. Did I feel deprived? Never. I had all the love a kid could ever need. One wonders how many affluent families today give their children everything money can buy, but give little of themselves.

When I was three or four, we moved to 4812-7th. Avenue, a walk-up cold water flat above Callucci's shoe store. Mr. Callucci and his wife owned and lived in the building. There was a Catholic school with an attached church and rectory across the avenue. As I remember, it was called St. Agatha. This is in a section of Brooklyn known as Bay Ridge and was a Norwegian enclave at the time. It may still be.

Just a few blocks away on Seventh Avenue and Forty-fifth Street is Sunset Park. It had two big beautiful public pools that I learned to swim in.

The roads were surfaced with a blacktop that was more tar than macadam and so soft they sometimes bubbled in the summer. Seventh Avenue had some traffic, but the side streets very little. It was great for stickball and roller-skating. The skates we had were clip-on wheels that mangled your shoes. The wheels could be put on a two-by-four with a box in front and you'd have transportation.

Stickball was played with a broom handle bat and a Spalding, a rubber ball that would bounce high and could be hit a mile, or at least to a couple of sewer covers spotted down the center of the streets. Unfortunately, a few windowpanes fell prey to them as well.

As kids we didn't have organized sports. We got sent out to play with the other kids and had fun. We didn't have teams; we just chose up sides from the kids who were out. You have to wonder if today's kids are under so much pressure that fun is harder to come by.

I was playing on the kitchen floor when I heard FDR's famous "this day will live in infamy" speech on the radio after Pearl Harbor. I remember mother crying. My Uncle Ralph graduated from a trade high school shortly thereafter and enlisted in the Coast Guard. Father avoided the draft because of me and because he had gotten work at the Brooklyn Navy Yard, a major shipyard during World War II. How he got the job is something worth telling.

He stood around in front of the gate and watched the men getting ready for work. Then he got a bag of tools and stood with them, watched what they did and did the same. What courage! He wasn't going to let the lack of a little training get in his way.

My father always had two or three jobs. After the war he got on with the Pullman Company, repairing railroad cars. He didn't know anything about that either, but he did it. He did odd plumbing jobs; I was his young helper on a few. After the Pullman Company closed its doors he hired on with the New York City Transit System, repairing subway cars. I helped him study for the written test.

The hell of it was he was a terrible mechanic. Mind, as I think back now he was tremendously artistic and talented in so many other ways. I'm sure that, given the education, he could have done almost anything. He certainly took care of his family.

I went to St. Agatha through the fourth grade. My parents considered themselves Catholics but they did it their way. They weren't regular churchgoers. Weddings and funerals drew them to church, but not much else. I was baptized, though, and had my first Communion, but my parents didn't beat religion to death.

Mother went back to the Pilgrim Laundry for a time when we lived on Fourth Avenue. Ann Donnellson, who lived across the hall, kept an eye on me for a few hours a day. Mrs. Donnellson's husband was in the Merchant Marine as was Jerry Maze's father. Jerry was my best friend.

Going to Catholic school, as I look back, was kind of a special experience. Discipline was rarely a problem when the teacher was a nun dressed in a black habit with her face framed in starched white. We learned the catechism along with the three Rs, in what was truly a caring environment, although on one occasion a nun pulled my hair. I told Mother when I got home and, sure enough, the next day she took me to see the nun and told her that it was never to happen again. If she had a problem, she was to call Mother and not touch me. She never again did.

Radio shows were the thing. After school we'd go out to play, but I'd always make sure I got home for the afternoon kids' radio shows—the Lone Ranger and Superman particularly. My first flights were with a kitchen towel cape and long leaps into the air before landing on the sofa. I didn't get much distance but often got a lot of air. The Lone Ranger, his Indian sidekick Tonto and his horse Silver created fantasies that shaped part of my childhood.

The homework got done but, unlike today, they didn't give kids much. Kids these days worry about "performance" and grades from kindergarten on. When do they get to use their imagination, fly like Superman and ride with the Lone Ranger? Computer games don't do that; they encourage isolation and nearly all of them glorify violence. The hardest thing to come by is an original idea, yet we're stifling our children's imagination.

Mother also loved the movies and it was truly the heyday of motion pictures. They were advertised on billboards in store windows; some of those billboards would be wonderful collectors' items now. The movie theaters had a dish night when for the price of admission, plus perhaps a few cents more, you got a dish that could grow to a full set over time. Father didn't care for the movies but Mother and I went every week. Part of the deal was to stop for an ice cream sundae after the show. In the winter, that made for a really cold walk home.

One show stands out in my mind, "10,000 B.C." or some such. It had dinosaurs and the director's idea of early mankind. This was when filmmaking was an art form without pyrotechnical effects or computer graphics. What fun.

****

To own your own home was the American dream and after World War II the economy went into the consumer mode and returning GIs used their benefits to buy homes in the suburbs. Levittown and its look-alikes sprang up all over the country. Father didn't want to move to the country; he just wanted his own house in Brooklyn. Sometime around 1947 he was doing a plumbing job for somebody and learned that a house on Dahill Road was on the market for a really good price. Without consulting Mother, but rather as a surprise to her, he went to see the place and put down a ten-dollar deposit. Mind, he didn't have much more than that to back it up, but by scraping and borrowing he came up with the small down payment. They were fifty dollars short at the closing, but a loan from the realtor saved them. Father was a homeowner.

The house, at 59 Dahill Road, abutted P.S. 230's playground. I entered fifth grade there. The playground was a rectangle with corners occupied by three houses surrounded by a tall hurricane fence. Our house was in the middle. On the other side of the fence from our backyard there were basketball courts and the back wall of the school that served as a great backdrop for stickball. A large electric sign advertising a lighting fixture store, also an abutter, provided some light for the basketball courts at night. The major section of the playground was given over to a softball diamond.

The fence that surrounded the three back yards jutting into the playground was a good twenty feet high; too high to climb but perfect for both softball and stickball home runs. I wound up with the largest collection of balls in the neighborhood.

The neighborhood's ethnic makeup changed from Norwegian to Italian/Jewish. The Flatbush Jewish Center on Church Avenue and Ocean Parkway, a five-minute walk from home, hosted the local Boy Scout troop. Mr. Myerson was the scoutmaster. He owned the fresh fish store across Church Avenue from the center.

It was an active troop with weekly meetings, Scout training and frequent weekend overnight camping trips. Summer camp was at Ten Mile River in the tri-state area of New York, New Jersey and Pennsylvania. I never had enough merit badges to become an Eagle Scout, but I did become an Explorer and an active leader in the troop.

My friends Harold Rosenfelt, Herby Kaye, Melvin Zuck and others were all Jewish. Man, did we eat well! From their parents I learned about gefilte fish, liver and onions, bagels with salmon and many other great dishes. At my house they pigged out on pasta and meatballs and even snuck a piece or two of pork.

Airplanes were never far from my mind, however, and building model airplanes was a passion. I wasn't that artistic a builder. I wanted models that flew. That required money and jobs to earn it. One job I had was delivering the *Brooklyn Eagle* newspaper. Although I didn't realize it as a kid, that was a notable paper in its day. The job didn't pay much and the bag was heavy as hell, but I got tips.

I also ventured into business—the shoe shine business. The corner on the intersection of McDonald Avenue and Church Avenue was a Mecca for foot traffic. It had subway entrances, a bank and two or three newsstands with people always coming and going, especially during rush hours. Certainly all those men should have shined shoes and I figured I was the one to provide that service. With some technical advice from my father, I put together a shoebox, determined a reasonable price and set up shop on the corner near the bank. Well it is said that most start-up businesses fail and mine was no exception. It was amazing how people could tolerate dirty shoes! I made a few bucks, enough to buy a little engine that I needed for a U-Control model I had built, and that was it.

Flying U-Controls was how I met Jerry Desmond, who was a few years older. He lived across East 2nd Street from Harold Rosenfelt. By any standard, Jerry was a childhood genius; he was also more than a little bit nuts. He was an only child and I'm confident his parents felt that a blessing. They lived in a little third floor railroad flat that he pretty much dominated. He had an upright piano that he could play extremely well, a chemistry set that would scare Saddam Hussein, and of course he built model airplanes.

He also was deeply interested in astronomy and built his own six-inch reflector telescope. He used a carpet roll tube and ground his own mirror. It was great. The Moon, the rings of Saturn and the moons of Jupiter became real. The only trouble was the streetlight in front of his house. Its light obliterated the night sky. The fix was a BB gun and a good eye.

From Jerry's lab also came magnesium flares that were sent aloft on a balloon filled with stove gas and a lit fuse. They created magnificent novas and I'm sure an interest from more than one concerned citizen.

And we talked. Where would a straight line end? What is infinity?

What is rational? Is there a God? Simple stuff like that. As I said, Jerry was brilliant. I have no idea what happened to him. After I started flying real little airplanes at age fifteen, I lost touch. But I figure Jerry is either heading up a NASA or nuclear physics program somewhere, or playing great music at some institution.

The house on Dahill Road was a two family; the upstairs apartment was rented and we lived on the first floor. We had a kitchen, a bathroom, two bedrooms and a living room. None was large. When my father's mother died from heart failure, my aunt Pauline was still living with her on 4th Avenue. She was seventeen. My parents had her come and live with us. She was beautiful and still is. My father and all of her other siblings have passed on. Pauline taught me how to dance the fox trot and the lindy while listening to the radio. She also took me to the Paramount Theater to see "Samson and Delilah" starring Victor Mature.

Pauline was married to my uncle Steve Covello at Father's house. Mother, who had become quite a seamstress, made her wedding dress.

My aunt Mary, who was older, also came to stay with us for a while. She married Uncle Joe and, yes, Mother made her dress too.

Mother worked on a White Sewing Machine that she cherished. She had a clientele who would come to our house for fittings. Her deal with Father was that the money she made would be spent on decorating. And boy, did she decorate. This was long before credit cards. Neither of my parents ever had one. If Mother saw a piece of furniture, a knickknack or a bolt of cloth for drapes that she liked, she'd put a few dollars down on it. The store would put it aside and she'd pay it off over time. She had great taste and her furniture still stands proudly in our New Hampshire home.

My uncle Ralph survived the war intact and served as a full-time station keeper at Floyd Bennett Field in the Navy Reserve. He later retired as a Chief Petty Officer. After the war, Floyd Bennett was a busy Naval Air Station and Ralph excelled as an aircraft mechanic. He married my aunt Marion and in short order came cousins Ralph (Skipper), Phyllis, Rusty, Ronnie and Ricky. They lived for quite a while at Navy housing next to the base. At least once a week mother and I would take a bus that ran down Flatbush Avenue to Avenue U and then transfer to a Green Line bus that would drop us right at the base housing gate; it was just before the Marine Parkway Bridge.

If Father was off, we would go by car. Mother never drove in her life. Father loved his cars and he loved to drive. He had a series of cars that he bought cheap and kept running on a wing and a prayer. Many an evening we'd pile into the car and go for a hot dog at Nathan's

Famous in Coney Island. Cars would be parked in front of Nathan's three or four deep. The hot dogs were the best in the world, nothing like today's Nathan's conglomerate frozen stuff. They were the real thing. Nathan's also sold frozen custard that was real custard. It was delicious, but you had to eat it quickly. Unlike today's plastic soft ice cream, custard would melt and run down your arm.

Full of hot dogs and custard, we continued our ride along the Belt Parkway. At that time the Belt was lit with sulfur lamps that produced a yellowish unreal light. It wasn't unusual for me to fall asleep in the backseat—well fed, safe and secure. What better foundation for life? How many children today in this land of plenty are in fact impoverished?

After a time, Ralph bought a house on the GI Bill in Levittown, about thirty miles out on Long Island. There were also some relatives closer in that we'd go to visit. These trips became adventures. Father was a great driver but knew nothing about maps and he had a proclivity to turn the wrong way. When I started to fly, he marveled at how I could find my way.

My grandfather Manginello continued to live alone on Reeve's Place but was a frequent presence in our home. I'd always know when he was there by the trail of Italian cigar smoke he left in his wake. When I got on with Mohawk Airlines, one of the captains I flew with smoked them and it was like being home again.

Grandfather also liked his wine, as did my father, who always kept a pretty serving bottle chilled in the refrigerator and before that the icebox. One time on 7th Avenue grandfather was carrying a gallon of red and fell coming up the stairs. It took several stitches to close up his nose but the wine bottle was safe!

Grandfather couldn't speak English very well, nor could he read or write. When necessary, he would sign with an X and a witness. My parents spoke Italian to him, but unfortunately never to me. Consequently, I know only a few words of Italian. My grandfather could play the concertina, a squeezebox with a few keys. It now has a place of honor on our mantle. In later years, after he suffered a heart attack and couldn't work any longer, he and I shared a room. I called him *paesano*, countryman in Italian.

Then there were Aunt Maggie and Uncle Joe Cicone, my father's uncle. Uncle Joe had a dry cleaning business that grew to be a small chain as his sons got older and helped him to branch out. Mother and Aunt Maggie got to be good friends and over time the two couples made some vacation trips together. They had the first TV set in the family and dinner and TV with them on Saturday nights was a ritual. There were only a few shows broadcast, all live: The Texaco Comedy Hour with Milton Berle and wrestling. Gorgeous George was king of the ring. The set was small, as they all were then, and the room dark as a couple of hours passed in a heartbeat. Before long we got our own set, a Garod. It burned tubes out like crazy, no transistors yet, but it worked.

****

Sometime around 1951, a Civil Air Patrol (CAP) Unit came to the area and was looking for kids to join. The CAP is an Air Force auxiliary that is active in search and rescue with light aircraft and their owners. During the war, they actually sank a German submarine off the Long Island shore. I joined, got my uniform and learned to do close order drill, salute and all that stuff. One of the officers was Captain Frank Mancusso, who owned a Cessna 170 that he kept at Deer Park Airport in Deer Park, Long Island. His brother Lou owned and operated the airport.

One weekend Captain Mancusso took a couple of us kids out to Deer Park for a ride in his airplane. It was my first ride and I was in the right seat that had controls. He let me wiggle the wings and fly it straight and level a little bit. I absolutely loved it! Operations and the repair hanger attached smelled just like my room. We used the same dope. They used it to treat the fabric that covered most of the small airplanes and I used it on the linen paper on my models.

Lou Mancusso operated a small fleet of Piper Cub J-3's in a flight school. Lou was a gentleman's gentleman and, like most of the pilots who either taught there or just hung out, he was a veteran pilot of World War II. He also ran a tight ship. If you weren't serious, you didn't fly there. The price of lessons was $13 an hour for dual and $8 for solo. You had to be 16 years old to solo with a Student Pilots License and a Class 3 Medical Certificate from the Civil Aviation Administration (the Federal Aviation Administration was yet to be born).

Although it would still be some months before I turned 16, Lou said that if my parents approved I could start taking lessons. I was hooked. From that moment on, I lived and breathed flying. It also meant that I'd have to work every available hour of every day until I finished high school to earn money to pay for the training.

I quit the CAP and dropped everything else to find time to go to school, work and get out to Deer Park Airport via the Long Island Railroad and a healthy hike. I went out early Saturday morning and came back Sunday evening. Lou gave me some work as a line boy, pumping gas and cleaning up. The Alexander Carpet Company based a twin engine Beechcraft Model 18 at the airport. It had about three acres of aluminum skin that had to be kept bright with Never-Dull cleaner. The job paid well, but it was tough work. John Donnelly, the mechanic, also threw that type of muscle work my way.

There were a couple of places where I could get a bed for the night. One was in a room behind a local bar. It was kind of noisy but as a kid I could sleep anywhere. In a pinch, Lou would let me sleep in operations. One night I woke up with a .38 tapping me on the nose. A patrolling police officer thought I had broken in. Fortunately, Lou was home and he got me off the hook.

I had progressed through the New York City Public School system without distinction; I did what I had to do to pass, no less but not much more. After 6th grade, I went from PS 230 to Mother's old school, PS 130, and then for one year to Montauk Junior High. In the 1950s, New York City had an excellent public school system. My high school, Erasmus, was one of the best. It was like a small college campus on Flatbush Avenue near Church Avenue. It had a center quadrangle with a statue of Erasmus, who was a Dutch scholar and theologian in the 15th Century. It was nicely landscaped with walkways surrounded by the school facilities. Different high schools in the city were noted for their specialties, Brooklyn Tech for engineering and Erasmus for liberal arts.

The school was crowded so they ran a split session, which was great because it gave me time to work after school. I started school at eight and was done by two.

My first job in high school was for Gary's Jewelry. Gary was a watchmaker when there still was such a thing, and had a small shop that carried jewelry and also sold money orders. He was physically handicapped with one leg several inches shorter than the other, which required a big metal brace. I'd help clean the jewelry in an acid solution, wait on customers for money orders and help out in general. Gary was a kind and generous person, as was his wife.

At ages fourteen and fifteen there was a lot going on. My parents bought and moved to another house, 535 East 3rd Street. It was several blocks away from Dahill Road, on a quieter street deeper into the Jewish community. The house sat on a double lot, had a driveway that led back to a garage and a porch with a shading evergreen the width of the house. A stonemason had built it of brick and it was a beauty. The only trouble was that as a single family home it would have been hard for them to carry the mortgage.

Father floated a Federal Home Administration (FHA) loan and turned it into a rear entrance two family. They lived in the first floor apartment with the front entrance from the porch. There was a kitchen/dining area, a living room, a bedroom, all of them big rooms with high ceilings, and a small bathroom. Also, there was a basement with an earthen floor used for the laundry, a workshop area and storage. Father later finished off a section of that as well.

I slept on a foldout couch bed in the living room until, shortly after moving in, Grandfather suffered a heart attack and moved in with us. He got the foldout and I moved to another couch mother made up as a bed. It worked out fine, particularly as I was spending more and more time away from home.

Puberty was a time I'll never forget and it left me with tremendous empathy for adolescents and mental illness. I was never so disorientated and frightened in my life, before or since. The doctor said it would pass and of course it did. He prescribed some Valium that made me feel worse than ever, so I didn't take it. This had nothing at all to do with sexual fantasies or any thing like that; it was the dirty work of hormonal change.

You only get to do puberty once, so it never came back. In my effort to understand what was happening to me, I became something of a psychology student and in balance that knowledge made me a better person. Now in public life, I am frustrated at our country's lack of support for treatable mental illness and our callous approach to adolescent education. I had the support of loving parents, but how many are lost to teenage suicide, school murders or simply thrown on the human scrap heap?

I had some other teenage problems as well. Thanks to Mother's concern that I never be underfed, I was always a little chubby. My hands also tended to be unsteady. None of that contributed to the John Wayne persona that I really thought I'd need to be a hotshot pilot. Guess what, I'm still chubby and my hands are still not rock steady, but it worked out just fine.

****

I can't tell you how many times over the years I've heard how lucky I was to have known what I wanted to do in life at such a young age. Let me tell you, I'll never discount luck, but be assured you'll always be a whole lot luckier with hard work and determination. In any case, I didn't know if I wanted to be an airline pilot. As much as I loved airplanes, I didn't know if I had the talent or if it paid well. If I had learned anything at all it was that being poor sucks. Those decisions came well after my first lessons at Deer Park.

Frankly, I don't think I'd choose to be an airline pilot today, nor a doctor, lawyer, teacher or any other professional. Contemporary America has turned its back on them and society seems senselessly beguiled with self-destructive social values force fed to us by the political far right. If I were young, I think I'd dedicate myself to fighting the bastards and recapturing the heritage that made being a professional a worthwhile goal.

In any event, I got my first big break in transportation as a Western Union bicycle messenger. It fit into my split session at Erasmus perfectly. I started after school and worked until the office closed at ten. The money was great and there were tips. In the early fifties, fax and e-mail didn't exist. If you needed a hard copy quickly, you got it through the Western Union telex system and a messenger.

Our office was just off of 13th Avenue, first near 39th Street and later around 46th Street. There were one or two guys with cars but most of us were kids with bikes. My bike was a Raleigh three speed, a noble steed. The deal was that rain or shine, snow or whatever, we went.

Our shift communicator was also our dispatcher. He physically composed the messages off the machine and put them together into routes that spread us out most efficiently. We were responsible for a radius of about five miles, quite a distance on a bike. We all had lights on our bikes, but outwitting the cars could still be pretty dangerous.

Our regular dispatcher was a huge man, probably in the five hundred pound range. He came to work with a case of Guinness Stout and a case of a pale beer and by the time he closed they were all gone, and yet I never saw him drunk. He was also fair to the kids and well liked.

Sadly, we were at war with North Korea and some of our messages were the "we regret to inform you" ones from the War Department. Usually the family knew before we delivered the hard copy, but it was still tough. The war ended a year or two later with an armistice promised by President Eisenhower. That was before I graduated from high school, but I always thought of Korea as my war, as it would have been had it continued.

My first flying lesson was in a J-3 with Joe Paulsen as an instructor. Joe worked part time for Lou and full time as a conductor for the Long Island Railroad. In a J-3, the student sits in the back and the instructor in front, reason being that the aircraft could only be flown solo from the rear seat because of weight distribution.

The Piper Cub began life around 1930 as the Taylor E2 powered by a tiny (20 horse power) Brownback engine and grossly underpowered. William Piper bought the company in 1931 and continued making derivatives under the Taylor banner until 1937, when Piper adopted his own name for the company and the J-3 was born. When the United States entered World War II, thousands were built for the US Army as the L4. The version we flew was technically the J3C65, signifying it had a (65HP) Continental engine driving a wooden two bladed fixed pitch propeller.

The J-3 had a wingspan of 35'3" and was 22'3" long. It weighed 640 pounds empty with a maximum takeoff weight of 1,100 pounds. The service ceiling was 12,000 feet. It carried 12 gallons of high-octane gasoline in a tank that hung down behind the instrument panel of the front seat; the fuel gauge was a rod through the fuel cap on a float. The engine burned about four gallons an hour at a cruising speed of about 75 miles per hour, providing a maximum range of about 250 miles. In World War II, tens of thousands of pilots got their initial training in the L4. The aircraft was simple, inexpensive and did everything right. If you could fly a J-3 well you could move up from there to fly anything. As a line check pilot with the airline, I often wished I had a J-3 to take a pilot back to fundamentals that had gotten lost with all the technology.

Joe Paulsen was a super instructor and that first 50 minutes in the air went by in a no time. I got to turn in both directions and fly straight and level, or at least try to; you have to develop visual cues and constantly cross check the altimeter and the compass. We'd do our air work in a designated practice area northeast of the field. A few miles from the airport there was a large state mental hospital to help find the airport. Joe let me find the airport but I wasn't ready for landings yet. That would come soon though.

Head In The Sky

The next step would be to work toward a private pilot's license that would enable me to carry passengers at age 17. I would do that but only as a step toward a commercial pilot's license, an instructor's rating and an instrument rating. For that I'd have to be 18 and accumulate about 250 flight hours and quite a bit of additional training.

About that time, my parents on one of their meals-on-wheels runs to me at Deer Park had a heart-to-heart with Lou Mancusso without me around. Their question: Did I have the ability to do it? I don't know what Lou said, but they went away convinced that I did. Bear in mind, it would still be another year before I'd be old enough to get a limited rural driver's license.

Even working every hour that I could, it would still be tough to pay for all that flight time. With my father's help I came up with a scheme to buy a J-3 with a 65 horsepower Franklin engine that was for sale in the area for $800. I figured that I could pay back the loan over two years and still fly a lot cheaper than renting an airplane. First National City Bank gave father a loan for the money and I was to pay it back and I did. What a wonderful thing for my parents to do. That was a lot money in 1952 and it took a lot of trust in me for them to do it.

I kept the airplane at an outside tie down at Deer Park and even slept in it. It was a good ship but not a cream puff. The engine would tend to quit at idle if you weren't careful and the fabric was pretty tender. But boy, I put hours on that bird. It couldn't have been that bad or the instructors wouldn't have flown with me. At least I don't think so.

My J-3 Cub

Some stuff wasn't so wonderful. One fellow in his own airplane had his engine fail after takeoff, tried to turn back to the field and was killed. Two other fellows had a small war surplus wooden twin-engine aircraft they were working toward a multi-engine rating in; we called it a bamboo bomber but I don't know what it actually was. They also crashed on takeoff, killing them both. That photo made the front page of the New York Daily News, showing their charred bodies in the cockpit. Sickening.

I no longer went to church and considered myself an agnostic. It was a deliberate decision based more on personal responsibility and disbelief in dogma than displeasure with the Catholic Church. I was never an atheist, just unwilling to accept another's perception of a God figure. Much later in life, after meeting my second wife Sue, I became a Unitarian Universalist. If I was to deal with death as a young person, my concept of God had to be mine, not somebody else's.

The only problem was most people don't know what an agnostic is and it's a little hard to spell; by comparison, being a UU is a piece of cake. Truth is there are many Unitarians who are agnostics and even atheists.

Once I started flying, visits to Ralph at Floyd Bennett Field were fun. Ralph would get me a pass on base and I'd spend the day with him. I'd help him run up the Twin Beechs, sit in the F-6s that were still around and meet his buddies. That paid off big time a little while later, when he connected me with a few guys in the Link room. I got my entire Link instrument training compliments of the US Navy.

Navy Twin Beech at North Field, Guam at the end of WWII
Note: Hellcats and Corsairs in background

Photo by Harold E. Gronenthal

It's funny how certain memories stay with you. A senior male English teacher made a comment I've never forgotten. One of the kids was complaining that his test grade for a writing piece was unfair. The teacher responded that life is not fair. In other words, get over it and move on. Good stuff.

On or about my 17th birthday, I took the required flight test and got my private pilot's license. I could now carry passengers and my first was Mother's lifelong friend Helen Mullen. Helen was a big lady and getting her into the back seat of the J-3 was a stitch. But she was a hot ticket and my airplane was up to the task and off we went. We flew around a little bit, landed and then it was Father's turn. Neither he nor Helen had ever been up in an airplane before. Father got a little airsick, but he was all right. Mother, on the other hand, drew the line and would not go.

About this time, another Italian kid by the name of Charley Giampa started flying out of Deer Park. He was from the Bronx. We were about the same age, which was kind of nice. He had a younger brother and a mom at home; his parents were divorced. Once my parents and I had dinner with them at their apartment. They lived on mean streets and I remember my father worrying about his car.

One weekend I took him along in the J-3 up to the Boston area, landing at the Revere Airport northeast of the city. We spent the night in the airplane and started back the next morning. Somewhere around Waverly, Rhode Island the engine lost power. It didn't quit altogether, but would only turn at about 1,500 rpm, not enough to maintain altitude. Part of primary training was always to have an emergency field in mind. We practiced on the potato farms that were part of the Long Island landscape in the 1950s, pulling up just short of landing.

But this wasn't a drill. I chose a farm and planned the approach to land with the plowed rows. I shut the engine down completely, both as a safeguard against fire and in the hope that as we slowed the prop would stop in a horizontal position and not be damaged if we nosed up in the soft earth. You can land a J-3 at about 40 mph and I did, rolling out probably no more than 100 feet. No damage. The only problem was we were in the middle of a big field. We set off for what looked like the farmhouse and found the farmer and his wife. It worked out that we were the third airplane to have paid them a visit, the last killing the pilot. Apparently he hadn't landed with the rows and it didn't work out too well.

The farmer pulled the aircraft off to the side and we took our few things out of the cockpit. As I remember, he even lent us train fare back to New York, where my father picked us up.

Now I was in a tight spot with a broken airplane sitting out on a field in Rhode Island and almost no money to do anything about it. Well, God came through for this agnostic young fellow and produced a hurricane that trashed the J-3. The insurance company totaled the aircraft and I wasn't faced with the expense of repairs. How's that for luck? Anyway, I repaid the farmer's loan and as a gift sent them a set of dishes Mother picked out for me. I'm sure he painted a big arrow on that field, pointing to his neighbor's farm.

Now in the market for a new airplane, I found a Commonwealth Skyranger, which had a side-by-side two pilot cockpit and was powered by an 85 horsepower Continental engine. It was manufactured in Canada, but not many were ever made. It had a simple electrical system and lights, making it possible to do instrument training and night flights.

My Commonwealth Skyranger

I gave this one a name, The Wanderer, although it never got painted on. Charley and I might have bought it as partners, I've forgotten. Either way, it makes no difference. Charley was killed off of Rockaway Airport to the southwest of Idlewild. By this time, Lou Mancusso had sold the flight school and Charley was flying with one of the new owners, who was also killed. It was theorized that their airplane had gone through the wake of a heavy aircraft landing at Idlewild and they had lost control.

His wake was a terrible ordeal, his mother clubbed with grief. All of us from Deer Park paid our respects, but it was tough. Charley had suffered massive head trauma, well beyond any mortician's skills of reconstruction, yet they had an open casket.

****

The next step up was a commercial pilot's license, for which I had to be 18 years old. I passed the written tests months ahead of time and also studied to qualify for instructor and instrument ratings. It was important that I start getting paid while gaining experience and flight instructing was a great way to build flight time. There was a lot of training going on. Zahn's Airport, where I would eventually teach, had an enormous flight school.

By tradition, flying at night was self-taught. Deer Park had only one paved runway. It was 2,200 feet long with no runway lights. On the west side of the field, there was a road that had a few lights on it; one was at the extended end of the runway. By lining up toward that light on the magnetic heading of the runway you could get within landing light range of the runway, although my one landing light on the Skyranger had about the candlepower of a good flashlight.

I would start making takeoffs and landings at dusk and just keep going. There weren't enough visual cues for depth perception, so I made the approach just above stalling speed, with enough power to have a gentle rate of descent and when I landed, I landed, grateful that the runway was there to meet me. After that I'd go over to practice at Zahn's, which was only about 20 miles away and had runway lights.

It was pretty scary stuff. Single engine night flying is dangerous in any case. Unlike daytime, there is no ability to find a field for an emergency landing as I did in Rhode Island. Pilots flying military single engines have parachutes. Normally, we didn't. I was careful to stay fairly close to an airport. As they say, there are old pilots and there are bold pilots, but no old bold pilots.

The way I was able to use the Skyranger for instrument training was really a hoot. It only had one attitude instrument, a turn and bank indicator (T&B). But you could do it with a T&B, an altimeter, a wet compass and a clock with a sweep second hand. I also wired in a low frequency range receiver and a primitive two-way radio.

In order not to see out with a safety pilot on board, I taped blue see-through plastic on the windows and wore orange goggles. It worked like a charm; you couldn't see a thing outside. Unfortunately, the safety pilot couldn't see much either! For the check ride, I wore a hood, because no one thought the CAA check airman would be that courageous.

Low frequency radio range stations were still in use and I used one located near Bridgeport Airport in Connecticut to practice low approaches. The way low frequency range stations worked was to array four transmitters in a diamond, two broadcasting an A (.-) in Morse code and two broadcasting an N (-.). Where the signal overlapped, the (.-) and the (-.) you heard a solid tone, so the station had four legs. When you passed over the station array, there was a cone of silence.

The big guys would have an Automatic Direction Finder (ADF) for orientation, well beyond my pocketbook. You could do it by listening to the volume of the signal and by mathematically determining what leg you were on by flying headings. In actual bad weather, low frequency range approaches could be made down to a minimum ceiling of 400 feet and one mile of visibility.

There were a couple of airline pilots who really helped with my instrument training and preparation for the commercial and instructor check rides. Fran Daley became a true mentor. He was a captain for American Airlines based at LaGuardia. He owned a beautiful home in Cold Spring Harbor on the North Shore of Long Island near the town of Huntington. He also ran a side business trading in aircraft.

Harry McPhail, a Pan American captain, was another. He had a regular route from Idlewild to Johannesburg, South Africa that would take him on the road for a couple of weeks at a time. He would then have several weeks off and spend time teaching at Deer Park.

After one of the partners was killed with Charley, the surviving partner gave the school back to Lou who turned it over to Ken Garafalo. Ken was an old-timer in Long Island aviation, who, as a friend of Lou's, sometimes managed the office for him. He was also a designated flight examiner and would later take a full-time job with the FAA. Ken helped me a lot and brought the flight school back up to snuff.

Bringing this all together was increasingly intense and commuting from Brooklyn was burning up valuable time. With my parents okay, I decided to finish the last half of my senior year at Bay Shore High and live close to the airport.

I needed a car and a place to stay. One of the private pilots that owned his own ship volunteered an old Buick that hadn't moved from behind the family garage in several years. They lived near old Mitchell Field. By this time, I had gotten a junior driver's license that allowed me to drive in rural areas during the daytime only. We resurrected the car with a new battery, pumped up the tires and got it on the road, sort of. Hey, beggars can't be choosers.

Ray Nelson worked for John as a mechanic and was extremely talented. He had built his own experimental ship that he flew and was into the whole home built experimental aircraft scene. Ray and his wife Mary Ann had been renting a small house in Deer Park, when a gentleman who was building an experimental ship in his garage suggested that they stay at his house on the South Shore, rent free, in exchange for Ray's help. The gentleman was leaving the country on business for an extended period. It was a big house and the Nelsons asked me to stay with them for a while and I did.

Unfortunately, after a few months Mary Ann, who was only a few years older than me, started getting maternal. One evening I decided to leave, loaded my stuff in the Buick and went off to find a cheap motel room. It was dark and, sure enough, a local police officer pulled me over for having a headlight out. Seeing my junior driver's license, with its daylight only restriction, he took me to the station house.

After a telephone call and a brief explanation, both my parents set sail in the family Chevy to get me out. From Brooklyn, that should have taken no more than an hour and a half. Three or four hours later they finally found the police station and got me sprung. And that was only the start of the adventure.

The Chevy was no cream puff, either, and somewhere on the Southern State Parkway it threw a fan belt or something and was all done. By now it was getting to be daybreak and we were a long way from nowhere. A milkman on his way to work took pity, picked us up from the side of the road and dropped us at a bus station. Somehow or the other, we managed to get home. A distress call to Uncle Ralph got him on the road to pick up Father and me and we found and rescued the Chevy. It took another ride out to Bay Shore to pay the fine and recapture the Buick.

But I did graduate from Bay Shore, needing only a few courses to meet their criteria. Chemistry was one of them. It was a hard course, but the teacher was good and I got through it all right. Unlike Erasmus, Bay Shore High was surrounded by ball fields and sprawled over a large area.

The graduation ceremony was held outside and, joining the graduating class, I got my diploma. My parents, Uncle Ralph and Aunt Marion and Helen were there. I remember getting an electric shaver that I used for years.

****

By July and my 18th birthday, I was ready. I'd gotten a Class II physical required for a commercial pilot's license, passed all the written tests, had all the required flight hours and flight training and was recommended by Ken for the flight test. I picked up the flight examiner from the CAA district office at Zahn's Airport in my Skyranger and two hours later I was a commercial pilot.

The instrument-rating examiner was a designated American Airlines captain whom I picked up at Flushing Airport, across the bay from LaGuardia. It was a really windy day and the one runway at Flushing had a wicked crosswind. By then I knew that Skyranger pretty well. The landing was a beauty and the examiner noticed it. Good start.

We did the required maneuvers and flew up to Bridgeport for a low frequency range approach. It all went well despite the strong winds that are tricky for a ship as slow as the Skyranger, especially with the limited equipment I had to work with. I got an "attaboy" and an instrument rating when I dropped him back at the airport.

The flight instructor's rating was a little more complex. It was with an examiner from the Zahn's office who gave a comprehensive oral exam and required a personally prepared workbook detailing all the phases and maneuvers for primary flight instruction.

I worked hard on the book, detailing all the maneuvers and the aerodynamic forces on the aircraft with data and carefully drawn pictures.

Everything was fine except that the examiner disagreed with my turn analysis wherein I said that as the angle of bank increases the aircraft would require more power and the nose held higher above the horizon. Being smarter than the average bear, I allowed him to convince me and went on to fly a highly satisfactory check ride.

In a matter of a few weeks, I had achieved my goal of a commercial pilot's license, an instrument rating and an instructor's rating.

Incidentally, my turn analysis was 100 percent correct. A B-767 requires about two-and-a-half degrees nose up to maintain altitude in a 45-degree bank.

Now I had the credentials to build on but little experience. I was also too young to inspire a lot of employer confidence and I had a 1A draft card. Even though the fighting had stopped in Korea, the country still had a draft.

I sold the Skyranger and paid off the bank. Now I was a professional and would no longer pay to fly. I never have since.

That summer I got a job at the Zahn's flight school as an instructor. After each flight, you had to make an entry into the student's logbook that included you license number. Mine is 1290572. Once you earn one, it's yours for life.

Zahn's was a bustling school in the summer. There could be half a dozen J-3s in the traffic pattern at any one time. I enjoyed teaching and still do. If you really want to learn something, try teaching it to someone else. One of an airline captain's primary responsibilities is to train the crew, so teaching primary flying was time well spent.

Besides working at Zahn's, I taught private pilots in their own aircraft, those who either wanted more flight training or were working on an instrument rating.

As the summer ended, so did the job at Zahn's. They retained only a few of their flight instructors year-round. American Airlines Captain Fran Daley was great. He knew everyone and took me around to meet them in my job quest. I submitted applications to just about every airline in the world, including two nonscheduled airlines based in New Jersey. Meteor Air was based at Teterborough Airport and Modern Air Transport at Newark Airport. Fran knew both owners and personally introduced me. Both carriers operated war surplus C-46s, a twin-engine tail dragger considerably bigger than a DC-3.

Meteor didn't have anything but Johnny Becker, the CEO of Modern, took a shine to me. He had been a captain for Northwest Airlines and left to start his own airline. The surplus C-46s were dirt cheap to buy from the government and there was money to be made with them.

God, I sure wanted to fly them. Captain Becker had a little twin Aero Commander that he let me fly, but he wouldn't hire me to fly the line. The crews were away for weeks flying revenue wherever there was a buck to be made. He was wise enough to know that the mature ladies who worked as flight attendants would have screwed my brains out! Mind you, I might have died happy, but I think my future would have turned out a whole lot differently.

****

In the meantime, Fran arranged a few ferry flights for me out to Chicago. There was a big aircraft dealer there by the name of Graubart. Those ferry runs generated a few interesting flights. Late one afternoon, Fran called: They had a Piper Tri-pacer at Spring Valley Airport, about 60 miles upstate, that needed to get to Chicago right away. My father volunteered to drive me to the airport and we arrived at dusk. I had flown Tri-pacer's before, so that was no big deal, and the weather forecast for the flight was good. I didn't have much with me, though, just the necessary charts, a toothbrush and a change of underwear.

About 30 miles west of Toledo the aircraft blew the main circuit breaker and everything went totally dark. A nonsmoker, I didn't have a match or cigarette lighter and I sure didn't have a flashlight. It was totally dark, no instruments, nothing. What a dumb shit! Fortunately, the lights of Toledo were still visible and I found the airport and landed with no communications or anything else. That's where I spent the night. Once I had light, a simple circuit breaker was found and reset and everything worked fine. Never again did I set foot in an airplane without a working flashlight.

Another time I was to pick up a Piper Apache, one of the first light twins, at the Marine Air Terminal at LaGuardia and ferry it to Chicago. I had never set foot in one, but it had an operations manual and I was a quick read. Trouble was, this time the weather wasn't so great and, considering the weather forecast, I refused to continue beyond Harrisburg. It was my first command decision in the face of management pressure. Graubart really wanted the aircraft. But he got over it and many more similar decisions were to come in my career.

That job was fun. Graubart was actually a very dynamic fellow and I liked Chicago. He didn't pay much, but the experience was valuable.

Johnny Becker came through with my first great job. Avco Manufacturing based their corporate Lodestar in a hanger next to Modern Air Transport and he knew the captain, Bailey Case, well. Bailey's copilot, John Harkin, had been on loan from Allegheny Airlines and was going back. Was I interested? You bet I was!

Avco Manufacturing was a giant holding company with major interests in Pan American Airlines, American Airlines, Consolidated Vultee Aircraft Corporation, Lycoming Engine, and Crosley, to name a few. Prior to 1947, it was known as the Aviation Corporation and developed and built thousands of B-24s and the famous PBY Catalina during World War II. Consolidated Vultee, popularly known as Convair, went on to produce the CV-240, CV-340 line of civilian airliners and the B-36 bomber. The Convair Division of General Dynamics would go on to be a major participant of the American space program.

In 1959, the name changed to Avco Corporation and in 1985 the company merged into Textron, Inc. It was a complex financial empire that antitrust laws would eventually force to divest.

Our boss, and the brains behind it all, was Victor Emanuel. Being available to him was our first responsibility. Essentially, Bailey and I were on call 24/7 on a moment's notice.

The Lockheed L-18 Lodestar was a transport version of the World War II Hudson bomber. It had two 1,200 horse power Wright 1820 Cyclone nine cylinder radial engines, driving three bladed variable pitch propellers. The same engine was used on the DC-3 and powered some of the Navy's WW II fighters. The military version had a crew of three and carried 14 passengers. We had a crew of two and perhaps half as many plush seats. It was not pressurized, nor were any of the other ships used as corporate aircraft after the war. Of those, the Lodestar was probably the most popular. It had a comfortable cabin and cruised at a respectable 200 mph. There was a Howard conversion of the Lodestar that had bigger engines and went faster.

Other aircraft used as corporate ships were the DC-3, B-23 and the B-26. The DC-3 was comfortable but slow, cruising at 150 mph. The B-23 was a bomber version of the DC-3 that lost out to the B-17 and never saw service as a bomber. Not many were made but after the war quite a few were converted to corporate aircraft. General Electric had a fleet of them based at White Plains Airport. They had bigger engines and cruised at about the same speed as a Lodestar.

Some corporations used converted B-26s that were about a hundred miles an hour faster but not very comfortable. The Martin version was called the Widow Maker because so many inexperienced pilots were killed trying to fly it.

At a gross weight of 21,000 pounds, the Lodestar was my largest aircraft to date. My first training flight with Captain Case was off runway 22 at Newark. He lined us up, locked the tail wheel, and said it was all mine. Holy shit, what a ride! All propeller driven airplanes must contend with torque. While the prop goes in our direction (on American engines the prop turns counter clockwise), the airplane wants to go in the opposite direction, to the left. I was totally unprepared for the torque from those big props and we zigzagged to the left and then overcorrected to the right before getting the goddamn thing straight. Those stubby twin tails had almost no authority until you accelerated to about 80 mph. It was a characteristic that could and did kill people.

Confederate Air Force Lockheed Lodestar

Photo by Gary Chambers

I grew to have tremendous respect for Bailey. He was an excellent pilot and a great commander who ran a highly professional cockpit. He set a standard and example that I followed throughout my career. Quite a guy.

Victor lived in a penthouse on Park Avenue in Manhattan and also had a home in Ithaca, New York. So we had a frequent run up to Ithaca, but we also took him or other senior executives all over the country. We flew some interesting and influential people. One time we had Vice President Richard Nixon on board. Mr. and Mrs. Hertz, of Hertz Rent A Car were friends of Victor's whom we frequently flew back and forth to Lexington, Kentucky. Invariably, Mrs. Hertz gave me a bag of fried chicken to take back to Victor. That meant a trip to Park Avenue. I have no idea if he ever ate it.

It was wonderful experience. I checked in a couple of hours before flight time, checked the weather, did the flight planning and the aircraft pre-flight. I also went to the local flight kitchen or caterer to pick up coffee and finger sandwiches. We didn't serve hot meals because we had no way to keep them warm.

I never flew the aircraft with the boss or senior executives on board. I did the copilot's job and served the passengers. Victor was a nervous flyer. He would have a soft drink and go through a box of tissues swabbing sweaty palms. I think he knew the track record for Lodestars, which wasn't that great.

Those small tail fins were responsible for two accidents that I knew of: On takeoff from LaGuardia, one Lodestar ran off the runway into a hanger, killing everyone on board. A buddy from Deer Park had another; he lost it at Meig's Field in Chicago. The strip is built out into Lake Michigan. He ran it into the lake. Fortunately, he survived, but they fired him.

We knew Michael Todd's crew. Shortly after he produced the epic movie "Around the World in Eighty Days," he and the crew crashed because of engine icing. All were killed. Those engines were very susceptible; the carburetors would ice up in a heartbeat if you didn't keep the carburetor temperature up. There was also an alcohol injection system, but if the engines iced up you were pretty much screwed.

After I was with Avco for about seven or eight months, our ship, N777W, was traded for a new upgraded version of the Lodestar manufactured by Lear at Santa Monica, California. It was called the Learstar. They took the same airframe and really cleaned it up aerodynamically. The cockpit was a sleek plastic shell and the engine cowlings were improved. All the avionics and aircraft systems were modernized. It was truly like a new airplane.

Bailey and I spent about a month out at the factory with our chief mechanic during the final phase of construction. They treated us like royalty, putting us up at Merriam Davies' old mansion on the beach. When we traveled, it was always first class. That's the way

Bailey wanted it and Avco seemed to go along. Bailey introduced me to Teacher's Scotch whiskey and filet mignon—pretty high off the hog for an eighteen-year-old from Brooklyn.

After the ship was rolled out, we did acceptance flights with Lear's chief test pilot, who was a character. He was a TWA captain; I think he still worked for them while at Lear. He told stories about Howard Hughes and having to fetch TWA Constellations from airports where Hughes had left them forgotten. The aircraft flew beautifully, with much better performance than the Lodestar. One day for kicks the test pilot feathered one engine and flew by a slower moving American Airlines CV-240. With the engine facing the Convair shut down and the prop streamliner to the slipstream and not turning it was an impressive sight.

The Learstar also held more fuel and had an upgraded integrated oxygen system that prompted us to attempt a nonstop Santa Monica to Newark flight. In order to do it, we would have to be up high and on oxygen for most of the trip. We made it in about nine hours.

That aircraft had another interesting feature: In precipitation that would produce static electricity like St. Elmo's fire, the plastic bubble around us would glow blue and our hair would stand up.

Within a few months after getting back, the jig was up. The bean counters at Avco had discovered my age when they reinsured the ship and were aghast that I had only turned nineteen years old. It was great while it lasted and Avco's glowing letter of recommendation served me well in the future.

Within a couple of years, Bailey would be gone as well. Apparently the ship had an autopilot problem and Bailey cranked in a little too much rudder and nearly twisted off those little freaking tail fins. He got the aircraft down safely but they let him go.

The lessons were clear: 1) An airline pilot is a professional making money for the corporation; a corporate pilot is chauffeur. 2) No matter how good you are, an employee without collective bargaining power is disposable.

Back to looking for a flying job, I updated all my airline applications. A pilots' employment agency at Teterborough was processing pilots to fly C-46s for the French fighting in French Indochina (Vietnam), but I wanted to get experience, not dead. Pan

American was hiring a small class and my Avco link got me an interview with the chief pilot at their Idlewild hanger. He was very encouraging and got my hopes up. He scheduled me with a group to take the Stanine Test that they and many other airlines used as an employment guide. It was a half-day test that had been developed by the Army to filter out pilot applicants who only wanted to stay out of foxholes.

There was no failing grade, just comparative scores, and there were absolutely no questions directly related to flying. At my age, based on such a curve, I was bound to score comparatively low and I wasn't chosen. In truth, I don't know if the test had anything to do with it, but who knows? I do know that a few years later I took the same test and was accepted as an Aviation Cadet in the US Air Force.

Applying at Eastern Airlines really pissed me off. They had what they called a personality test. What it really did was allow them a reason to discriminate against minorities and women. Discrimination was widely practiced in the airline industry. There were no blacks or women and very few Jews or Italians. It would take years and President Lyndon Johnson for that to change. I wrote Eddie Rickenbacker a letter and told him what he could do with his airline. He never answered. Rickenbacker was a World War I ace who ran Eastern from 1938 until 1959.

As it worked out, after being hired by Mohawk in 1959, an airline that didn't discriminate, I had an uninterrupted career until I retired. Had I gone with either Pan American or Eastern, my job would have vanished when they went out of business.

Interlude: Learning Some Nuts And Bolts

Although I had no luck finding an airline job, my Lodestar experience helped me get on with Walsh Construction as a copilot. They operated a corporate Lodestar out of White Plains Airport in Westchester County, New York. The captain was Fred Leslie, who needed a replacement for the co-pilot/mechanic who had left for another job. He knew I wasn't a mechanic but needed someone in the right seat in any case.

Walsh was and still is a large national heavy contractor that was doing work on the St. Lawrence Seaway at the time. The seaway would open a deep water shipping route from the Atlantic Ocean to the Great Lakes. Work began in 1954; it would be 1959 before the seaway opened for traffic. It was an enormous earth-moving project involving the construction of locks. Walsh worked on the Eisenhower locks.

We made frequent flights to Massena, New York on the St. Lawrence, about 15 miles from the job. A few times we tagged along to look; it was a huge project. There were also frequent flights to Montreal and Chicago. Unlike Bailey, Fred ran a frugal budget. Instead of Teachers and steak, it would more likely be the chicken special and maybe a beer.

47

Fred was a good guy and a good stick, but unfortunately they really needed a co-pilot/mechanic who could do at least routine maintenance. After four or five months I was let go.

On leaving Deer Park, I went back to live with my parents, sharing the living room with my grandfather. While banging out applications, I found some work teaching instrument flying in private aircraft at Teterboro, but it was a frustrating time and I was beginning to feel like a bum. That was around the time that Arthur Godfrey of radio and TV fame got busted for buzzing the Teterboro tower with his DC-3.

I took the time off after flying for Walsh Construction as an opportunity to go to Queens College at night. Queens College, located in Flushing, is part of the City University of New York (CUNY). Former Secretary of State Colin Powell, born in Harlem and just a couple of months older than I am, went to City College within the CUNY system. The CUNY colleges were inexpensive and topnotch. I took courses for a few years but didn't accumulate enough credits for a degree.

Back then most commercial pilots, airline or otherwise, didn't have extensive college educations. That would change. In later years, many had their master's or even doctorates. Had my job search not ended successfully at such a young age, I'm sure I would have continued my college education as well. I really enjoyed it. But I certainly got an advanced education. The airline spent hundreds of thousands of dollars on training in my thirty-eight years of service.

With a good word from Johnny Becker, I got an interview with the Northwest Airlines' chief pilot in Minneapolis, Minnesota, their main base. They gave me a pass to fly from Idlewild on one of their Boeing 377 Stratocruisers, which was a civilian adaptation of the Boeing B-29 Superfortress. Pan American, B.O.A.C. and Northwest operated them for quite a while after the war. Although the B-377 held only about 100 people, it was the biggest airplane I'd ever been on and it seemed enormous.

The chief pilot said Northwest had pilots on furlough and wasn't hiring any at that time, but they had a class for transportation agents starting right away, with openings at Idlewild. Was I interested? What the heck, why not? I said "sure."

The course would take about a month. At Northwest, a transportation agent was trained to do just about everything, from weight and balance to working the ticket counter. The training was absolutely wonderful and gave me an insight into the operation of an airline that a pilot would never get otherwise. I certainly didn't plan to stay on as an agent, but the pay wasn't bad and the experience would be great. Plus, they might eventually hire me as a pilot.

They put the guys up at a YMCA in St. Paul. I found the town loaded with young people who had migrated off the surrounding farms to work. Sure enough, I met a farmer's daughter at a popular cafeteria and we dated a few times. She took me out to the farm, where I saw my first pig. They didn't have pigs at the Prospect Park zoo.

Now you have to understand, my dating experience was just about nil. Not out of lack of interest but because of lack of time and opportunity. Boy, what a surprise. This gal could kiss. She had a tongue like a serpent. Much to my chagrin, my virtue remained intact, but I'll never forget the farmer's daughter and my training at Northwest.

Northwest shared a temporary Quonset hut with Pan American at Idlewild. The welfare gate had swung open and the great Puerto Rican immigration to New York City was in full swing. Pan Am always had the terminal jammed full with passengers going to and from the island. The air-conditioning wasn't great and the smell of garlic (even for me, an Italian) was almost overpowering at times.

But it was fun. Most of the time I worked the ticket counter, which was interesting. There were no computers and we wrote tickets for lengthy international itineraries by hand, reserving the seats through Northwest reservations by phone. Some of the tickets cost thousands of dollars. Sometimes I caught a break and worked on the ramp parking aircraft.

After about three months, I quit the job at Northwest. My draft status was killing my chances for an airline job and I knew I had to do something about it. The New York Air National Guard had an attractive Aviation Cadet program. If you qualified as a U.S. Air Force Aviation Cadet, you went through Air Force Flight training, which took about eighteen months, and served the remainder of your three-year enlistment with the Air National Guard at Floyd Bennett

Field. That only required one weekend a month and a two-week summer camp.

I took the Air Force exam at Mitchell Field on Long Island. It was still a military base but not too many years later would be turned into a huge shopping mall. The test was an expanded all-day version of the same Stanine Test I had taken with Pan American. This time there was no problem and I was accepted. After undergoing a stringent flight physical, I was inducted as an Airman Basic in the Air Force Aviation Cadet program.

All of this took months. I did weekends at Floyd Bennett as a clerk's helper and attended the summer camp at the Air Guard's compound adjacent to the Syracuse Airport. The Guard deployed from there. That was cool. The enlisted guys paid to rent an airplane from the fixed base operator and I gave them all rides.

At that time, the unit was changing over from B-26s to F-94 jet light attack bombers. The F-94 was a souped up T-33 trainer with a bite. After summer camp, our pilot class was ordered to report to the Air Force flight school in San Antonio, Texas. The report date was about three months away. I had quickly learned that you do a lot of waiting in the service.

About two weeks before we were set to go, we got the word. The brass had figured out that there were two seats in the F-94, the pilot and an armament officer. They didn't have any armament officers and they wanted us to change schools and do that. Well, when inducted we had a contract with the Air Guard specifying that we were enlisting only as Aviation Cadets. Therefore, we had a choice whether to accept the training they were offering or not. I chose not.

So, after consuming almost a year, my military career came to an end. By this time, I was all psyched up, so I was disappointed, but I sure as shit wasn't going to be a passenger in that freaking airplane, no matter how important the job.

On the plus side, I had an honorable discharge and was no longer subject to the draft. I was a member of an inactive Air Force Reserve unit and could be activated, but just about every other airline pilot was in the same boat. I certainly didn't need to go through primary and basic flight training again.

So out went more applications explaining my new draft status. I sent the Federal Aviation Administration (FAA) an application for a flying job, too. The FAA was established in 1958 and had replaced the CAA. Back came a letter from the FAA with an offer to train as an air traffic controller; they were looking for additional staffing in the New York area. The school would be for six weeks at their big training center in Oklahoma City, all expenses paid. The training sounded great and I accepted.

Not long before, I had met my wife to be, Carol Friedlander, in an English composition class at Queens College. While I was in Oklahoma City, she would be in San Francisco on an extended visit to her aunt and uncle—perfect timing.

The school was comprehensive, including: air traffic control separation standards, radio procedures, radar procedures (as they existed at that time), weather, and a host of other things. All the students had some background, most as military air traffic controllers. It was pretty demanding and some flunked out, but I did well.

Three or four of us rented a small furnished house to cut expenses; we were only paid a small per diem. They were nice guys, two of whom went with me to New York Center. (Years later, I was saddened to learn that one had committed suicide.) During the training, they chipped in to rent an airplane a few times and I took them sightseeing.

We graduated, got our air traffic control certificates and went to our respective stations. Mine was New York Center, then located at Idlewild Airport. It would later move to just outside MacArthur Airport on Long Island. Our next task was to memorize different areas that they controlled. We were apprentices and it would be a long time before we would be directly responsible for separating air traffic.

It was a good paying job with government benefits and a twenty year retirement program. My prospective father-in-law thought that was great—at last I had a real job. He didn't think much of that flying stuff.

I wasn't at New York Center a month when I received a letter from Mohawk Airlines asking me to report for a pilot class in Utica, New York on November 2, 1959. I'll always remember the date because it was my date of hire. And it left me with only three days notice. My decision was made in seconds: Go for it! When I left my New York Center job, I learned that in the fine print of my school agreement with the FAA I had agreed to work for them for at least for six months. Otherwise, I would have to repay them for the training. That was accomplished at rate of $10 a month over many years, but it was still a good deal.

Moving Up With Mohawk

On November 1st, I headed up the New York Thruway in a Volkswagen Beetle and west of Albany ran into a hellacious snowstorm that lasted the rest of the way to Utica. What the hell was I getting into? It was only the first day of November and the weather was terrible. As instructed, I checked into the downtown YMCA that airlines seemed to have an affinity for and met a couple of my classmates who had arrived earlier. Ours was a class of about ten; a prior class had started two weeks before.

A few years earlier, the City of Utica had built Mohawk a big new hanger with office space to entice the airline to move its home base up from Ithaca. Mohawk had its roots in Ithaca from its start as Robinson Airlines in December 1946. Robinson was an intrastate state airline that flew Twin Beeches. The name was changed to Mohawk Airlines in 1953 with CAB approval and the DC-3 became their ship of the line. In 1955, Mohawk bought a handful of Convair 240s from General Claire Chennault's Civil Air Transport (CAT), which operated under the Flying Tiger insignia. By 1959, Mohawk was expanding its route structure wherever the CAB would let them and was operating more Convairs, including CV-440s, which were somewhat larger.

Utica was also changing from being an infamous mob hangout to going straight. There was a notorious FBI anti-racketeering bust just a year or two before I got there. The city was still pretty rough in 1959, with strip clubs and the like.

Our introduction to Mohawk started bright and early with paper work. For the first year as a new hire, we would be on probation and paid a flat rate of $400 a month, plus a 22 cents an hour meal expense when away from base on a trip. A representative of the Airline Pilots Association (ALPA) explained our contract with the company and emphasized that during our first year we could be terminated at the company's discretion. Several were.

Unlike the maritime, ALPA does not have a national seniority list; your seniority number is with the airline you work for and carries no significance with any other airline. That seniority number is tremendously important because it determines bid awards for base assignment, equipment and flights. Our date of hire would be November 2, 1959, the day we reported, and our seniority number would be added to the present list. It was determined by birth date within our class. I wound up last with a seniority number of 100. I joked that it would take me over thirty years to be number one on the list. By that time, the airline would have merged with others, changed its name several times and grown to have more than 6,000 pilots.

Others in my class were: Bob Knapp, Paul Kinack, Clay Collins and Arnie Atkatz. Bob went up the management path to become Senior Director of Flight Operations. Arnie was an excellent instructor who eventually checked me out in the BAC-1-11. Tragically, after retirement he killed himself. Many years later, Paul was again a classmate of mine in B-767 training. These are a few of the fond memories I have of some of the men I worked with for almost forty years.

A silly thing I remember about Clay Collins happened when we shared an apartment in Rome, New York before I was married. Clay had a wife and kids and $400 a month didn't go very far even then. He had taken the last eggs out of the refrigerator to cook and somehow he went down on the floor and the eggs went up. He survived, but the eggs didn't. We sprang for beer and pizza that night.

Wally Ott from maintenance taught us the nuts and bolts of the DC-3. That was our first assignment.

Douglas developed the DC-3 for American Airlines to use for transcontinental sleeper flights in the United States. It flew for the first time on December 17, 1935, and it became the mainstay for US domestic airlines prior to World War II. During the war, 10,000 were built for the military as C-47s. Mohawk's had the same engines I had on the Lodestars, two 1,200 horsepower Wright 1820s. The maximum takeoff weight was 28,000 pounds. Ours held around 26 passengers, two pilots and a flight attendant. I'm sure I flew one or two DC-3s that were older than I was!

By today's standards, the DC-3 is a fairly simple aircraft, but a few aspects are tricky. It took Wally half a day to explain the operation of the hydraulic retractable landing gear. A sequence of something like three operations is required. It also had a high-octane gasoline heater to warm the cabin, which demanded high priority attention. The aircraft was unpressurized and the cockpit windows leaked like a sieve, so we had raincoat training.

Flight training requirements were nothing like they are now. Three takeoffs and landings were all the FAA required, and even those could be touch and go. Flight simulators were still far in the future, so all training was in the aircraft.

Walt Reed was our instructor, a good stick and a prince of a guy. Mohawk allowed more than the minimal three takeoffs and landings, so we got to do some air work and shut an engine down. We didn't do V1 cuts, engine failures at the most critical time on take off, in a DC-3. The airplane flew under an exemption from the FAA because it could not meet the criteria for an engine failure on takeoff.

Walt had three of us—Clay, me, and one of the others from our class. I flew first and found the DC-3 to be like a big docile balloon compared to the Lodestar. We did the air work and, before returning to the field to do the bounces, Walt had the other guys come up to have a turn. We were sitting in the back with Clay flying and all of a sudden the world began to turn upside down! Clay had only flown light airplanes before. So when Walt said to do an approach to a stall, Clay honked it back into a full stall. A DC-3 will go inverted in a heartbeat. As I said, Walt was a good stick; a lesser pilot wouldn't have recovered.

Mohawk DC-3 on the ramp at Rochester, NY 1960

Photo by Tom Kirn

That winter went by in a blur. We didn't fly DC-3s very high; they were unpressurized and were used on the shorter flights. Whenever possible we flew under Visual Flight Rules (VFR), which was allowable then. The captains knew all the landmarks and we were expected to learn them as well. It was latter-day barnstorming, but they were really good at it. The training was great. You learned to use everything at your disposal, visual cues and radio aids. But I only flew the DC-3 for a couple of hundred hours. By early spring I was moved up to the Convairs.

Consolidated Vultee, a division of my former employer, Avco Manufacturing, built the Convairs. The CV-240 held 40 passengers and the CV-340/440 could carry 52. The latter version was a few feet longer, had a bigger wing, and was aerodynamically cleaner. Here again, they were built to meet the needs of American Airlines, as a replacement for the DC-3.

All three versions had Pratt & Whitney R2800 engines, which produced about 2,400 horse power, the CV-240 a little less, the CV-

440 a little more, or so Pratt & Whitney claimed. Those of us who flew them didn't think so. The maximum takeoff weight of the CV-440 was 50,000 pounds, 8,000 pounds heavier than the CV-240. Few of us thought the aircraft would ever meet V1 engine failure criteria in warm weather at that weight.

Mohawk Convair 240 taking passengers and luggage the old way.

Photo by Tom Kirn

Mohawk Convair 440 taxing away from the gate at Newark Airport, NJ.

Photo by Bob Garrard

Jerry Sorlucco

The CV-580 was a CV-340/440 conversion to turbine engines that produced twice as much power. Although I never flew them, I know they never lacked power. In the 440s, I always felt we had our ass hanging out.

****

The Ethical Culture Society, off Central Park in Manhattan, married Carol and me on April 9, 1960. I was twenty-two and Carol nineteen. The reception was at the home of Carol's parents in Flushing, with both families contributing all kinds of goodies. We took the VW beetle to Washington, D.C. for our honeymoon and caught the tail end of the cherry blossoms.

It worked out that I had some time off because the flight attendants had gone on strike to get their union recognized by the company and the pilots refused to cross the picket line. Over time, there would be a lot of labor disputes at Mohawk that I would be intimately involved with. Fortunately, the flight attendant strike only lasted a couple of weeks and they won their union.

We went directly from Washington to Ithaca, where I had been sent on temporary duty assignment as a reserve first officer. The company put me up expense free at the old Ithaca Hotel downtown. That only lasted a few weeks. I returned to the Utica base and we rented a duplex apartment in New Hartford.

Number one daughter Karen was born at St. Elisabeth's Catholic hospital in downtown Utica on January 7, 1961. Which goes to show that inexperience in dating does not make you less reproductive.

When my probationary year ended, I had been flying the Convairs for quite some time and going on incremental flight pay meant a big salary increase. There was also an opening at the Newark base, which would be a whole lot closer to our families. I bid for it and got it.

Carol's parents put us up for a couple of months until we found a small house in Levittown that was in our price range, $16,500. We qualified for a four and a half percent FHA mortgage with a minimum down payment. We lived there for several years and then bought a house in Long Beach, which we shared until our separation in 1983.

58

Carol and I had two more children, both girls. Theresa was born on August 18, 1962 and Danielle on May 3, 1967. Dr. Saul Pastor, a dear friend and student whom I had worked with years before as a flight instructor, delivered both at Huntington Hospital. Both Carol and I have remarried, but we remain friends and share six grandchildren. We were together twenty-three years. She is a large part of what I am remembering in these pages and she always will be.

****

I flew as a first officer for about a year and a half, while many with the airlines spent half their career waiting to get into the left seat. The reason was that Mohawk doubled in size within a few years after I was hired. During that year and a half, it was possible for me as a junior copilot to fly with most of the fifty-odd captains who were with Mohawk from its start. It was a privilege. They rank among the giants who built the industry and, boy, they were characters.

Unlike today, in 1960 there was very little formal training. You learned on the job with mentoring. With our route structure we were up and down six, eight or more times a day in all kinds northeastern weather. There were no autopilots. The aircraft was hand flown from takeoff to landing. Unless the situation was unusual, the captains would split legs and share in the radio communications and other copilot duties. It was an intense relationship that the company relied upon for screening during the probationary year. About forty percent of our class was let go.

On average, we'd spend fifteen to eighteen days and nights away from home every month. I was not there for the birth of any of our children. Junior pilots work on holidays, so Christmas, for example, would often be on the 23rd or the 26th. Invariably, pipes would break and snowstorms happen when I was away. As I said earlier, there is a price for everything, and airline pilots and their families paid for the job in time apart and often divorce. Juxtaposed with being away from family was the closeness you developed with your crew. In the early days, pilots shared a hotel room and the stewardess (yes, they were called that) was expected to open the door for a late arrival from another crew. We only carried one flight attendant until the jets came. At the old Hotel Ithaca, we had a large room with half a dozen beds so that three pilot crews would bunk together, sharing one bathroom. The hotel had steam heat, so you went to bed roasting and woke up with ice in the hopper. The junior pilot got the bed under the window. Sometimes I woke up powdered with snow.

Try to envision yourself sitting within arm's length of someone for ten to fourteen or more hours a day in a space about the size of a closet. Imagine a view that's sometimes beautiful, often nonexistent. Then shake the closet frequently so hard that you can't read a wristwatch. Eat junk food off your lap and, until recent years, fill the air with smoke (the guys used to smoke everything but old socks). Now and again stage an event that scares the shit out of you. And you will have a pretty fair, nonromantic view of an airline cockpit. I figure I spent well over 30,000 hours or three full years there. It is a place of special professional friendships that I will always treasure.

****

I've used the terms copilot and first officer, which begs for a bit of explanation. As I have mentioned, the command structure that the world uses for aviation is drawn from the maritime. The captain is the commander; the first officer is second in command and so on down the line. Both the captain and first officer must be pilots, but for other flight deck positions they need not be. There used to be professional flight engineers and navigators but few if any remain; they were replaced by either technology or specially trained pilots.

Replacing professional flight engineers with pilot flight engineers was a debacle that lead to American Airlines leaving ALPA in 1963 to form its own union, the Allied Pilots Association. Prior to the jets, flight engineers were specially trained mechanics that kept the reciprocating engines and aircraft system running in the large four engine aircraft. In the early days, they also did maintenance at outlying stations. Because jet engines are actually simpler to operate, and as systems became more automated, ALPA converted the flight engineer position for its pilots.

The American Airlines pilots couldn't abide by that and bolted. At the time they left, ALPA represented every pilot on every United States certified airline. Now none of the handful of pilots' unions has true national stature and the profession is being raped more and more every day.

The old guys were colorful and they had balls. Most are gone now. As we say, they've taken their last flight west, the pathfinders. It was out of such great respect for them and our profession that I became active in ALPA. I knew from the first that only by standing together could we be strong enough to stand up for our rights and do the job entrusted to us safely. If I could give today's airline pilots anything from this memoir, it would be to know that they have a proud heritage: Don't be afraid of the fuckers who are destroying your industry. If you have the courage, you can stand up to them and change the tide.

****

Mohawk had three main bases – Utica, Newark and Boston. There was a small base in Utica and a satellite for a while in Detroit. Base stability was nonexistent, so some of the captains I remember flying with at Newark may have been out of Boston or Utica. No matter what the base, among those still alive and kicking, as far as I know, are: Dick Burdick, Frank Delmar, Paul Finnerty, Charlie Gordon, Bernie Krouk, Fred Manderioli, Jack Mozian, Tony Santorelli, Chub Trainor, Bob Zimmerman, Bob Burns, Nino Ciancetta, John Evans, Barney Fairbanks, Stan Graziul, John Hessel, Bob Jenkins, Jim Johnson, Bob Kaplan, Hank Meed, Bill O'Shea, Walt Reed and Ed Rooney. Fortunately, that is quite a long list.

I worked three months running with Jim Johnson, whom I was told wasn't the easiest captain to fly with. We got along okay. You learn from everyone's style, even those you don't wish to imitate.

Later in the year, I was deadheading home to Utica on his flight in a CV-440. It was snowing like hell with the wind blowing from the southeast and he had to circle from an ILS, a precision approach, to runway 33 to land the opposite way on runway 15. We did that a lot in those days. With weather minima of a 500-foot ceiling and one-mile visibility, it could be sporty.

Well, this one didn't work out too well. After touchdown and roaring into reverse, the aircraft left the runway into deep snow. The props and the front of both engines were torn off and there we sat.

There was no fire, but it was definitely time to leave. I went to the rear door, deployed the escape slide and invited the passengers to go first. The snow was so deep the slide wasn't a problem. I was in uniform so the passengers responded, but I never did see any of the crew. There was no impact, so I knew no one was injured up front. The terminal was only a couple of hundred yards away. Seeing no reason to witness the rest of the show, I threw down my bags, walked to the terminal and went home.

The next day I learned the flight attendant had been given a couple of weeks vacation with pay for doing such a great job evacuating the aircraft, and that a passenger had wondered why one of the pilots was sitting in the back instead of up front! I thought it prudent not to shed any further light on the subject and I was never asked about it. Last I heard, Jim was living in Florida and attending some of the retired Mohawk pilot reunions.

I really enjoyed working with most of the captains. Steve Gondek was a big gregarious man who was one of the founders of the union at Mohawk and did various stints in management. He knew just about everyone. One night, after making six or eight stops in rotten weather, we landed in Cleveland. It was my leg and we had a circling approach at minima to runway 18 in the snow. One of the tower chiefs met us at the gate and invited us all to his house to sample his home brew. Man that was a good batch, and the couch I slept on felt soft as a cloud. Steve died much too young of brain cancer in 1981.

Flying with Bob Gettman was like spending the day in the fog. He smoked those Italian black cigars that reminded me of my grandfather. He was a man I liked a lot and a good guy to work for. Bob died in 2000.

Captain Bob Burns was an older guy who whistled all the time. At first I thought he just found me too boring to talk to, but that wasn't true. He just passed the time by whistling. Whistle or no, he was a good stick and is living the high life doing slow-rolls in Florida. I'll give you odds he is whistling while he does them.

I flew with Dick Cunningham on one of his first trips in a CV-240. Dick had bid up from the DC-3. It was a wicked night in Buffalo, with drifting snow obscuring the taxiways. First thing you know were taxiing through deep snow drifts with the props throwing snow all over the place. I exclaimed, "Dick, Dick, this thing only has about a foot of prop clearance, it's not a DC-3!"

Dick was a big man who had a lot of children and was deeply religious. He was a neighbor of Nino Ciancetta, a senior pilot I would get to know well in ALPA work. As legend goes, he took it upon himself to speak to Nino's wife about his on-the-line behavior. Nino, being seriously pissed, shot Dick's station wagon with a bow and arrow. How many people do you know who have brought down a station wagon with a bow and arrow? Dick died a natural death in 1987.

They all had their quirks, but nobody gave them any shit. They were captains and woe to anyone who forgot that. By way of illustration, my friend Dave Phipps has a story of flying with John Wholley out of Boston. John was chief pilot at Boston for quite a while and an extremely professional and respected guy. Dave had done the pre-flight on a Convair and found one of the tires worn through seven of its ten layers. Captain John told maintenance to replace it and they groused that they would take a delay if they did. John told them to replace it. Well, after getting to the first stop half an hour late, they learned that they had been roasted on Bob Peach's morning briefing. Every day, Peach, the president and CEO, held a morning conference call to all the stations.

The next trip out of Logan, Dave reported to Captain John that they had a brand-new tire with the label still on it. Dave told John that he thought they weren't taking any chances. John ordered maintenance to replace the new tire! He then had the tire sent COMAT, company freight, to Bob Peach, along with a message that if one of his captains says to replace a tire it was to be replaced with no further bullshit. John knew how to make a point. He has operated a seaplane base on the Merrimack River in New Hampshire since he retired many years ago.

My first flight after being transferred to Newark was with Charlie Gordon. It was an 0 Christ hundred early flight and I made sure I was early. The operations agent told me Captain Gordon was the guy sacked out on the bench. I certainly didn't want to wake him up, so I just set about doing the flight planning and so forth. After a while, in comes a wiry cabin attendant who checks in for our flight and picks up the phone. She then proceeds to lambaste this poor person on the other end, who as it turns out was Charlie's wife! Charlie never moved a muscle or said a word. After a while he got up, signed the flight plan, and off we went.

That day he didn't say two words; I worked the radios but never flew a leg. The next day I flew all the legs and he worked the radios. Whatever else was going on in his life, he didn't let the small shit get him down and wherever he is I hope he still doesn't. He was a good pilot and I enjoyed working with him.

Captain Eddy Johnson was a piece of work. He came from Brooklyn and had cultivated the best Brooklyn accent and slang ever heard. But it was all a put on. I always knew deep down that Eddy could speak the Queen's English better than the Queen. It was his style; it instantly made him one of the boys and they in turn treated him like a king.

Eddy's best buddy was Dick Burdick; they were like night and day. Dick was a bon vivant and a ladies' man, although I think he also came from Brooklyn, so they had that in common. They were the original odd couple, a sophisticated Jew and one of da boys.

Fun aside, Eddy could fly. I was with him on a CV-440 flight into Newark on the tail end of a hurricane. The rain had moved out and the visibility was good, but the wind was howling from the west. It was my leg and I fought that airplane to earth like a bucking bronco. It was an ILS approach to runway 4R circle to land on runway 29. The turn to final is made over a railroad bridge and other structures that help to create ground effect turbulence. The landing was safe if not delicate earning me a "good job kid" from Eddy, which was about as articulate as Eddy got. But what a confidence builder for me; it was wonderful. In a very short period of time I would be the captain, with no one else to look after me, responsible for many lives and the training of my first officers. To me, those old-timers were the great ones and I am forever in their debt.

I also flew a lot with Irv Galle, both before and after I checked out as a captain. The reason why I flew with him after I checked out was that my seniority wasn't high enough to hold a reserve captain's slot. I would bid a block with Irv, fly one or two trips, and simply be used as a captain for the rest of the month at captain's pay.

Irv was a true gentleman. We shared an Italian background and we both loved good Italian food. Irv was a smooth pilot with a laid back and artistic style. After we had flown together a few times, he was studying for a six-month check ride and I loaned him a CV-440 manual I had purchased from Consolidated Vultee; the Mohawk manual was a piece of crap. The airline was under pressure from the FAA to tighten up its training department and that pressure was flowing downhill. Irv did fine and appreciated the help.

Irv also allowed me to fly from the left seat, which was permitted back then at the captain's discretion. The practice was stopped not many years later. Moving from right seat to left is difficult at first; your hands have to learn a different job. I learned later in check pilot training that moving back to the right seat was also challenging. But I loved it and Irv was one of the captains who made it happen for me.

He was divorced and first thing you know a pretty and sweet flight attendant named Gale was flying our trips. I remember one bitter cold morning at Idlewild. Gale was in tears. Her parents had lost their house in a fire. Irv was there for her, caring and responsive. A while later they were married and remained together until Irv's death in 1996. His son from his first marriage is now a senior pilot with US Airways.

****

In early 1961, Mohawk cut a deal with Eastern Airlines to purchase a portion of Eastern's Martin 404 fleet, along with some the New England routes Eastern had acquired with the purchase of Colonial Airlines several years earlier. This would add about eight new cities and a bunch of new aircraft, substantially increasing the size of the airline.

The Martin 202/404 series, like the Convair 240/340/440 series, was designed as a modern airliner to replace the DC-3. It had two Pratt & Whitney R-2800 2,400 horsepower engines and carried forty-four passengers with a gross takeoff weight of 44,900 pounds.

As part of the deal, Eastern provided training for a number of Mohawk pilots until we could get our training department up to speed. I was in one of the first groups to go to Eastern's Miami base for flight training. They put us up at a hotel near the airport. It had a great swimming pool that became study hall central. I'd never been to Florida before. Along with being hot as Hades, every afternoon showers marched across the airport and raised hell with training flights. There was also a minor bird in the hotel lobby that knew swear words in several languages.

Flight simulators still had not come along, so all training was in the aircraft. The Eastern instructor was a good guy, if not a little to the political far right. He was a John Bircher and talked about it a fair amount. We had been separated into captains and first officers when sent down by Mohawk, but the training for a captain was not that much more extensive. So I asked if I could do the additional procedures and get an Airline Transport Rating (ATR) from the FAA, as the captains would. I had already passed all the written testing that the FAA had recorded. The instructor agreed and that's what we did.

There are several things with the M404 that are unique: The wings have a lot of up swipe, or dihedral. It also has a walking landing gear so that the aircraft rocks forward with acceleration or braking. This supposedly reduces stress, but can also make for a wild ride when taxiing if you're not careful. There is an auto feather system like the Convair's to meet the requirements of an engine failure on takeoff; the one on the M404 would cage that.

Hairiest of all, the aircraft has two high BTU Janitrol heaters in each wing root to provide hot air to the wings' leading edge anti-icing system. They burn the same high-test aviation gasoline that the engines do. We had fire detectors for these but the unfortunate procedure for a fire was to land immediately, no matter what was below, because the wing was likely to burn off. I would think a lot about that not too many years later.

Single engine work out of the Miami airport was kind of neat. The M404 does not zoom aloft on one engine but rather labors for every foot of altitude. As we sailed off across the Florida Everglades struggling up, I could swear I saw alligators with their mouths open, calling us for lunch.

But the training was excellent and I got my ATR. I was certified a captain at the age of twenty-three. I'm certain that I was the youngest airline captain in America at the time. After I got back to base, I was one of just a few pilots to have a rating and I was flying trips as captain in short order.

Eastern Air Lines Martin 404 on display at the
Mid Atlantic Air Museum.

Photo by Sam Chui

****

We had moved from Levittown to Long Beach just a short time before I got my first assignment as a captain from crew schedule. It was a round robin from Idlewild up through northern New York State and back. I didn't sleep much the night before. Was I excited, anxious? You bet. I was a husband, a father, and a homeowner and in the morning would be in command of an aircraft full of people. That was a lot of responsibility for a young man and don't think for a moment that I didn't feel the weight.

As I said earlier, somehow you have to develop the ability to focus, eliminate negative distractions and thoughts, and be confident in your experience, training and ability. It is the mark and sometimes curse of professionals. It can easily be perceived as arrogance, aloofness or self-absorption. The shrinks call it compartmentalization. Many a spouse has simply called it being an asshole.

I've forgotten who the first officer was, or the flight attendant, but they were both older than I was. Once into the routine and checklist, everything went well and I settled down. As a new captain, I had higher weather minima and company policy required me to take off and land the airplane for the first hundred hours and not swap legs. The former was a Federal Air Regulation (FAR); the latter got a bit old and I thought deserved a little flexibility.

The weather upstate wasn't bad, but coming back to Idlewild we had a stop at Poughkeepsie, which was reporting poor braking action. With a full ship of passengers returning to the large IBM center nearby, dispatch wasn't keen on me overflying the station. Poughkeepsie had only one runway, which was fairly short, about 4,200 feet, as I recall. Braking action reports weren't very sophisticated in those days. It was usually someone running down the runway with a truck; if he survived, the braking action was considered better than nil – nil would automatically cancel the landing.

I said I'd give it a shot so long as the wind remained pretty much down the runway. The M-404 has enormous fowler flaps that when fully deployed allow a slow cross-the-fence speed of about 115 knots. Eastern had managed to break an airplane in half at Saranac Lake because the pilot had used full flaps with a high sink rate, believing he could just rotate the airplane and flare. The ship would rotate fine, but continue to drop like a rock without power.

Anyway, I touched down on the numbers and went directly into reverse prop pitch and allowed those big flaps to continue to provide aerodynamic braking. The book said to retract the flaps after touchdown to get more weight on the wheels for better braking. Bullshit. That's fine if you have the braking but, on a runway slick as a baby's bottom, it is better to use everything you have. I gave myself an A+ for airmanship and a D for judgment. It was stupid to land under those conditions. I was quickly figuring it out: As a captain, what you didn't do was far more important that how sharp a pilot you were. That's what those four stripes were all about – knowing when to say no.

The FAA changed the name of the Airline Transport Rating (ATR) to Airline Transport Pilot (ATP), which is more descriptive. For each aircraft that you operate as a pilot in command, or captain, you must have a separate rating listed on your license. They combine similar types, so the M-404 is bundled with the M-202, which is an earlier unpressurized version. By the time I retired, I had type ratings in the M-202 M-404, CV-240 CV-340 CV-440, FA-27 FA-227, BA-111, DC-9, B-727, B-757 and B767. One of our captains and a friend, Clif Magnor, made getting ratings a hobby and has one in just about every aircraft known to man. I was rated in the Convair shortly after becoming a captain and flew both it and the Martin, although the company did try not to mix the two types.

Mohawk had only one fatal accident with the M-404, in July1963. I heard the news on TV at the Hotel Fontainbleau in Miami; Carol and I were there on vacation. I learned from crew schedule on the telephone that the captain was Dick Dennis, whom I'd only met once or twice. They were taking off on runway 27 in Rochester and apparently were touched by a tornado shortly after liftoff. A hotel near the airport had all the pool furniture on one side only blown into the trees. We had weather radar on the Martin, but by today's standards it was primitive. The radar was not computer enhanced and had poor penetration; it would attenuate, showing only the leading edge of the weather. Unlike now, the airports had no weather radar at all, or any ability to report wind shear. Down the road, many accidents related to wind shear led to far better equipment and training to predict them, avoid them and survive them.

On the whole, the Martin was a good airplane. I had one engine blow a jug (a cylinder), which required a precautionary in-flight shut down, and one engine blew an oil line while we were taxiing to the gate. The single nose wheel had a weak steering fork that I had break twice, one just at liftoff from Utica and another on landing at Glens Falls. The incident on takeoff had me cross swords with a junior dispatcher when he suggested that since we were in-flight anyway, why not continue to the next stop? I perhaps unkindly suggested that he put a qualified person on so we could make plans for our return to Utica.

You never retract a damaged wheel into the wheel well. You may jam it in and not get it down again. On the other hand, if the landing gear is left down single engine performance is substantially reduced. In both instances, once the nose wheel was on the ground it spun, causing considerable shaking but no further damage.

As described earlier, the wing anti-icing fed off two Janitrol heaters in each engine nacelle. The cabin heat and windshield anti-ice were fed by two other Janitrol heaters in the wheel wells. You could keep the cabin real toasty and get the inner pane of the windshield hot as hell, but the outside still readily took on ice. In the process, your eyes would be fried! I remember having to hold to land at Elmira in icing and really taking on a load. We had little more than peep hole to see through and much more ice than I liked on the airframe and wings.

Ice will form as moisture or precipitation strikes the airframe and wing and tail leading edges. It will occur in a relatively narrow temperature range around freezing. Ice on the aircraft is dangerous stuff. It disturbs the airflow over the wings and tail. In reciprocating engines it can choke carburetors; in jet engines it can disturb sensing units and break off into the engine and cause damage.

Numerous fatal accidents have been attributed to the effects of icing. More than one crash has occurred on approach to landing, when the aircraft was slowed to a normal approach speed and landing flaps were extended. The horizontal tail stabilizer would stall and over she'd go. The smart pilot didn't use normal landing flap and carried more airspeed—to hell with the book.

Icing is dealt with in various ways. Reciprocating engines can route manifold heated air into the carburetors and the Convairs routed it to the wing and tail leading edges, if selected. The Lodestars, DC-3, FH-227 and many others used deicing boots on the wing and tail leading edges that pumped air pressure into expanding bladders to break the ice off after it had formed.

The jets have the advantage of an abundant hot air source – the engines. They also operate at higher altitudes and at high speed, which heats the skin of the aircraft by air friction. The jets don't glow like the space shuttle, which reenters the atmosphere at 17,000 miles per hour (25 Mach). But even at eight-tenths the speed of sound (.80 Mach) the skin rise is about 20 degrees centigrade. At slow speeds that doesn't happen, so they route hot air from a stage of engine compression to the leading edges. On the B-757 and B-767, only the wings' leading edges are heated. Boeing determined that the tail was safe without it.

I used one of my nine lives one winter day on a round-trip M-404 flight from Idlewild scheduled to go to Albany, Plattsburg, Burlington, Albany and return to Idlewild. The aircraft had been ferried into position earlier in the day from Utica, following a heavy maintenance check. Rusty McAdams was my first officer.

Rusty was an Irishman's Irishman. He'd flown in the military, been through a sad divorce and was a great beer drinking buddy. We'd had more than one or two together and I enjoyed working with him.

On those short hops, we never got up all that high and were always in the clouds if there were any around. We were picking up light icing and had the wing anti-icing on. The P&W 2800s burned about 100 gallons of high-octane fuel per hour times two, for an anticipated flight burn of about 200 gallons. As we approached Albany we noted that our burn was about 80 gallons higher. I had maintenance meet the aircraft and wanted it checked. Usually something like that would be a bad fuel gauge that could be determined by manually dip sticking the fuel tanks. The mechanic said the gauge was right. I told him to check the engines and wheel wells for a possible fuel leak. Again I got back, "Captain, I don't see a thing."

Back up again and in the clouds on our way to Plattsburg, we encountered icing again and again we turned on the anti-icing system. Now, of course, we were really focused on the fuel gauges. Sure enough, down she went and off the system went. We dropped to a lower altitude and held our breath until we landed at Plattsburgh. Now Rusty and I were out in the wheel wells with our flashlights and what a sight. Both wheel wells were inundated with fuel all over those goddamn Janitrol heaters; it was unbelievable that we hadn't blown up. The mechanic there found that the fitting on the heater fuel lines had only been hand tightened! He simply tightened the fittings and cleaned the wheel wells and we were on our way.

That mechanic in Albany was the only person I directly had fired in my airline career. He had violated a trust and I gave the company a choice – fire him or I would kill him the next time I saw him. We postulated that the only reason we didn't have an explosion was that the environment was too rich with fuel to ignite.

Rusty McAdams perished in an accident some years later while flying a FH-227 on approach to Albany in March 1972. His first officer, Bill Matthews, was also killed but, amazingly, the flight attendant and many passengers survived. The accident was attributed to a runaway propeller, causing them to land short and strike a house.

****

From 1938 until 1978, airlines and routes had to be certified by the Civil Aviation Board (CAB) through the authority of the Civil Aeronautics Act. The CAB grandfathered twenty-three airlines that became known as trunk carriers. The CAB set standard fares balanced between profitable and unprofitable routes.

Small, fixed base, non-transport carriers could provide service upon request on an unscheduled basis with aircraft restricted to a takeoff weight of 12,500 pounds. After World War II, Supplemental Air Carriers, or non-scheds, were given certificates of Public Convenience and Necessity (PCN).

Between 1945 and 1951, the CAB certified nineteen local-service airlines, or feeder lines. Among them were Mohawk, Allegheny, Piedmont and North Central; all later merged and became U.S. Airways. Pacific Southwest Airlines started as a California intrastate airline and was purchased by USAir in 1987, along with Piedmont. Some of the local service routes were subsidized.

When I was hired in 1959, the four-engine jets were making their first appearance. Pan American was the first to put the Boeing 707 in service in 1958, followed by United and Delta with DC-8s at the end of 1959. These aircraft held almost twice as many passengers and flew more than twice as fast.

It was the dawn of the jet age and the airline industry took off. The trunk lines focused on the big jets and establishing markets for them; the feeder carriers were able to strike deals and pick up their crumbs. The CAB wouldn't allow us to compete with the big guys, but there were still a lot of markets without air service and the result could be mutually beneficial if we brought traffic to trunks at the larger airports.

In that same time frame, the Vietnam War and the continuing Cold War with the Soviet Union formed the backdrop of the 1960s and my first decade with the airline. The Vietnam War is said to have started when John F. Kennedy pledged to help South Vietnam defend against the North in 1961, although this country had become unofficially involved there years before. The French colonial rulers of Indo-China before World War II had got their ass kicked at Dien Bien Phu in 1954 and the United States was afraid of a communist takeover of a region that included Laos and Cambodia as well as Vietnam.

After JFK's assassination in 1963, Lyndon Johnson dramatically escalated the war following his fabricated Gulf of Tonkin incident. By 1968, the United States had over 500,000 troops in Vietnam with the end of the war not in sight, although the Johnson administration knew by then that the United States could not win. Due to the unpopularity of the war, Lyndon Johnson chose not to run for reelection in 1968. I saw his "I will not be a candidate" speech in Albany on an over night.

After his election, Richard Nixon began to disengage with a Vietnamization plan in 1969. Ultimately, the United States signed a cease-fire agreement with North Vietnam in 1973. The North eventually overran South Vietnam in 1975 and Saigon fell.

United States casualties: 55,000 dead and a couple of hundred thousand wounded or traumatized for life; North and South Vietnamese casualties were in the millions. Cost to the U.S. economy was hundreds of billions of dollars. What's absolutely frightening is that this is now ancient history in the 21st Century and one has to wonder if we are forever doomed to repeat our mistakes. As this is written, the United States has devastated Afghanistan and conquered Iraq, and there is no end in sight.

Somewhat like my job with Western Union, I dealt with the aftermath of Vietnam. We carried hundreds of caskets on their final trip. Vietnam was my third major war and I wasn't yet 30 years old.

The Cold War with the Soviet Union grew out of the infamous Yalta conference at the end of World War II. Winston Churchill's famous speech at Fulton, Missouri, on March 5, 1946, articulated its start with the words "an iron curtain has descended on Europe."

On April 15, 1961, just months after JFK's inauguration to the presidency, CIA operatives and Cuban exiles launched an invasion of Cuba at the Bay of Pigs that ended in disaster. Khrushchev started to build the Berlin wall on August 13, 1961. Later, the Soviet Union's build-up of missiles in Cuba took us to the brink of nuclear war in the fall of 1962. The threat of nuclear war was excruciatingly real. I had first officers who had been Strategic Air Command (SAC) pilots and were aloft in B-52s armed with nuclear bombs when JFK and Khrushchev went eyeball to eyeball.

****

Juxtaposed with the horrors and social division of the war in Indo-China and the specter of the Cold War was the space program. The Soviet Union had beaten us into space by orbiting Sputnik 1, an unmanned capsule, in 1957. The United States responded by announcing Project Mercury on October 7, 1958. The objectives made up of six manned flights between 1961 and 1963 to: 1) orbit a manned spacecraft around Earth, 2) investigate man's ability to function in space and 3) recover both man and spacecraft safely. However, three weeks after Alan Shepard's short suborbital flight on May 5, 1961, President Kennedy announced the goal of landing a man on the moon before the end of the decade. Wow, did that captivate our national imagination!

For me as a young airline pilot, the jet age and the space age were one and it couldn't have been more exciting. Sure the military had been flying jets since the end of World War II, but jets in civil aviation and the space age dawned at the same time, in the 1960s.

The Gemini Program flew ten missions in twenty months from 1965 to 1966. They learned how to fly a spacecraft, maneuver it in orbit and rendezvous and dock with other vehicles. The BAC-111, the first twin-engine jet airliner, went in service at Mohawk in the spring of 1965. It was followed by the DC-9-10 later in the year at Eastern and Delta.

The Apollo Program began with tragedy on January 27, 1967, when Gus Grissom, Ed White and Roger Chaffee were killed in a fire during a plugs out test on a pad. The vehicle was redesigned and would subsequently fly 45 astronauts, starting with Apollo 7, in October of 1968, to Apollo-Soyuz in July of 1975.

On July 16, 1969, Apollo 11 made good JFK's promise to walk on the moon. Who can forget Neil Armstrong's phrase, "That's one small step for [a] man, one giant leap for mankind," as he set foot on the moon. It was such a defining moment that most people remember where they were; there was great TV and radio coverage. I was driving on the Meadowbrook Parkway with Carol and the kids returning to Long Beach. We had been out shopping. By then I was a BAC-111 captain and 32 years old.

It was such an uplifting time. As the astronauts were pushing the space frontier, I was at the forefront of passenger jet travel. The world was shrinking; we could now look at our planet Earth from space and travel the globe in only hours.

In all, twelve men walked on the moon, the last from Apollo 17 in December 1972. That was the last of manned space exploration. Since then all exploration has been by unmanned probes. Probes are safer and cheaper, to be sure, but not the same as having human beings in deep space. Space flight after 1972 would be confined to Earth orbit scientific and military missions.

Skylab, America's first space station, was launched into orbit on May 14, 1973, and was manned for over 171 days. There were three missions to it during the remainder of 1973, the last returning on February 8, 1974. The lab itself would reenter the Earth's atmosphere on July 11, 1979, scattering debris over the Indian Ocean, with some parts falling in Australia.

On the diplomatic front, the Soviet Union's spacecraft, Soyuz 19, docked with Apollo 18 on July 17, 1975. Optimists worldwide thought that just perhaps we wouldn't make the Earth uninhabitable due to a nuclear holocaust. Others of us still wonder. In any case, Russia and the United states continue to have an extraordinary working relationship is space.

After a six-year hiatus, the United States again ventured into orbit with the Space Shuttle Program. The shuttle is a recoverable vehicle that reenters the atmosphere and glides to a landing. The first space shuttle, Columbia, was launched on April 12, 1981. A fleet of five of them was built: Columbia, Challenger, Discovery, Atlantis and Endeavor.

Although the shuttle program has been highly successful and has contributed enormously to scientific research, there have been fatal accidents. On January 1, 1986, Challenger exploded seventy-two seconds after liftoff, killing the crew of seven. And on February 1, 2003, Columbia disintegrated during reentry, spreading debris over hundreds of square miles of Texas and Louisiana. Again, the crew of seven perished.

The technological spin-off from the space programs has been awesome and has touched everyone's life. It directly contributed to the jet age technologies in computers, simulation, navigation, flight management systems, system sensing, weather forecasting ability, metallurgy and communications, to name a few.

While I think humankind will always be an explorer and look up at the night sky in wonder, the decade of the sixties was special. It was when we actually went into space and went to the moon. Despite the other horrors in the world, the space program combined with the jet age and JFK's brief moment of Camelot to uplift our consciousness and give us hope. Just a few years into the 21st Century it seems we've traded that sense of wonder and hope for far-right political cant that has us looking to the past instead of optimistically looking to the future.

****

To its credit, Mohawk hired quite a few Vietnam veterans. One of them was Bud Dean, who became a dear friend and roommate in Marblehead, Massachusetts. Bud had been a Marine chopper pilot. I'd teased him that he'd never flown a fixed wing airplane in his life until he worked with me. And in fact the Marines didn't overdo fixed wing training if you went the chopper route. By the time he was with me, I was flying the FH-227 (more about the aircraft later). He always approached a landing at an angle so steep that I had to admonish him that I couldn't see the runway with my necktie in my face! His excuse was that in his last job he'd be shot at if he went in low. We worked it out. In 1965, Mohawk was the first American airline to get short haul jets, the BAC One Eleven. Built by the British Aircraft Corporation, the BAC-111 (series 200) was powered by two Rolls Royce Spey Mk 506 turbofans, each producing 10,330 pounds of thrust. The series 200 had a takeoff weight of 79,000 lbs and carried a flight crew of two, two flight attendants and 79 passengers. American Airlines would operate BAC-111 series 400s that had slightly bigger engines and a takeoff weight of 88,500 lbs.

Mohawk had them painted in "Buckskin" colors that were definitely impressive. And you certainly could hear them coming. God they were loud! Unfortunately, too loud for later noise criteria that would force operators to put noise suppressers on the back of the engines. They looked like garbage cans and reduced the thrust of the engine.

Mohawk Airlines BAC1-11 in "Buckskin" colors deplaning passengers at Newark Airport, NJ.

Photo by George W. Hamlin

The T-tail configuration caused a crash that killed the crew in its flight test program. The fuselage blocked the airflow over the tail in a stall, causing a "deep" stall, wherein the elevator didn't have enough authority to lower the nose, or the engine enough power to accelerate out of the stall. The aircraft literally pancaked to the ground.

BAC resolved the deep stall problem by installing a stick pusher into the elevator hydraulic control system. It would sense an impending stall early and push the yoke drastically forward while there was still elevator authority. Needless to say, you had to be careful not to fly too slowly close to the ground. It was kind of a jerk-off fix that pilots didn't like and I doubt that, with the wind shear recovery techniques that have evolved since, the aircraft would be certified now.

The DC-9-10 that entered service on Eastern and Delta later in 1965 also had a T-tail and potential deep stall problem that never caused an incident. The elevator on a DC-9 is normally controlled by mechanical linkage to flying tabs that move the much larger elevator. However, if the yoke is pushed full forward hydraulic pressure is introduced directly to elevator servos that move the elevator itself with more than sufficient authority to lower the nose.

The DC-9-30, a larger aircraft, would enter service in 1967, as would the Boeing 737-100 and 200. They would have larger cabins and be more comfortable, but the BAC-111 was first.

It was a nice flying aircraft with a low altitude wing that restricted the aircraft to a low Mach number, but that wasn't a big factor for Mohawk. The aircraft did not have drop-out passenger oxygen so we were restricted to an altitude below 25,000 feet anyway.

The controls were powered hydraulically with a "manual reversion" ability. That meant that if you had the arms of a gorilla you could fight the ship to earth, which made for great sport in the simulator. It was also a stumbling block for female pilots trying to get a toehold in the industry. That was solved when the FAA ruled that one pilot could ask the other to help with the muscle input.

Still on the downside, the ship had a weak generator/starter system. BAC incorporated the two functions in a single unit that demanded blood from both. Also, the single chemical lavatory in the rear amounted to little more than a smelly litter box when serving over eighty people.

On June 23, 1967 another fatal flaw would surface on a BAC-111 that had departed Elmira, New York. Destructively hot gas from the

Auxiliary Power Unit (APU) in the tail stove-piped up the vertical stabilizer and burned through the hydraulic and mechanical control lines, rendering the ship completely uncontrollable. It crashed into a hillside, killing everyone on board, including Charley Bullock, the captain, and Troy Rudesill, the first officer.

Investigators determined that a valve that was supposed to prevent that channel of hot gas flow hadn't closed properly. The valves were upgraded and use of the APU in flight was no longer permitted.

The radio communications and cockpit voice recordings from the flight crew were heartbreaking. Mohawk CEO Bob Peach was said to have reacted very emotionally, which is not surprising. He might been happier as a robber baron in the 19th Century, but he was a passionate man.

I was too junior to bid the One Eleven for a couple of years and would fly the FH-227s when they came in 1966. The company was eager to move to an all turbine fleet with upgraded avionics as soon as possible. Trouble was, there were few choices available at that time. There were several conversions to the Convairs that replaced the reciprocating engines with turbine engines, the most popular being the Convair CV-580. Allegheny went that route, settling on the 3,750-shaft horsepower Allison 501-D13H turboprop driving a four-bladed constant speed propeller. It was the same engine that powered the Lockheed Electra. They also had some Fairchild F-27s.

Mohawk went with the Fairchild Hiller FH-227, which was manufactured in Hagerstown, Pennsylvania. Fokker, a Dutch company, developed the original F-27 in the early 1950s. Fokker had an agreement with Fairchild to build the Friendships in the United States. Fairchild developed the FH-227 independently. It had a maximum takeoff weight of 45,500 pounds, a flight crew of two and held 52 passengers. It was powered by two Rolls Royce Dart 5327L (2,300shp) turbine engines that drove a Dowty Rotol four-bladed propeller.

Although the ship did have an autopilot, upgraded avionics and engines that ran like a sewing machine, I thought the aircraft was a piece of shit. The props had a propensity to run away and were a factor in Rusty McAdams' fatal accident. It was underpowered and to save weight had a pneumatic system (rather than hydraulic), which was totally unsuitable for cold New England weather. Pneumatic systems attract moisture and freeze.

It was also the only aircraft I ever flew that required full elevator trim under heavy landing weights; that's a serious indication of aerodynamic instability. Under crosswind conditions, you'd be hitting the rudder stops to keep the aircraft straight.

Mohawk Airlines Fairchild Hiller FH-227 taxing to the gate at Newark Airport, NJ.

Photo by Bob Garrard

The extremely high-pitched noise the props made on the ground made most of us deaf, including me. Contributing was a period when the company insisted on one-engine stops, which was a stupid and dangerous procedure.

Mohawk lost another FH-227 one wintry, blowing night on November 19, 1969. Investigators found that Ray Hourihan and his first officer John Morrow had become disorientated during a VOR approach to Glens Falls and crashed into a mountain near Lake

George, killing all aboard. Who knows? Ray was thought to be a good pilot.

The FH-227 also became a centerpiece in two labor disputes that directly involved me. The first had to do with Ralph Colliander, whom Peach had elevated to vice president of flying. Colliander had been very active in ALPA work, particularly in contract negotiations, until he developed diabetes, which cost him his first class medical certificate.

Colliander was also pretty tight with the then President of ALPA, Charley Ruby, a captain from National Airlines. In the background was a push by Mohawk to operate Twin Otters in a scheduled air taxi service called Air North. Twin Otters, weighing less than 12,500 pounds, did not fall under Federal Air Regulation (FAR) 121, nor did the CAB control them. It was said, although never substantiated to me, that Ruby had an interest in such a service elsewhere. My position and that of the Mohawk Master Executive Council (MEC) was that the traveling public and the pilots would not be adequately protected.

It is important to understand that at that time every scheduled flight in America was controlled by the CAB, with the protection of operating under FAR 121, and every pilot in scheduled service had the protection of a union. What was being forced on the traveling public and down our throats was a substandard level of service reminiscent of the 1920s!

The Mohawk MEC tried to buck the tide with no success. I remember being at an ALPA Board of Directors meeting in Miami and visiting every other airline's MEC and pleading with them to take the scheduled air taxi issue seriously and to support us in controlling it on a national level. We weren't against smaller, perhaps more efficient aircraft for small markets; we just wanted the same level of safety and protection for the public and the pilots. The guys at Pan American, TWA, Eastern, Braniff and National couldn't be bothered. They were flying the big jets and could not have cared less about little Twin Otters flying around in upstate New York. Well, guess what. Those airlines are no longer in business because those little shit box airplanes grew to be more efficient commuter fleets that were still not flown by union pilots. All that led to deregulation in 1978 and a cutthroat industry in which the traveling public has every reason in the world to fear for its safety.

So it is not hard to see why Peach wanted Colliander and his buddies at the ALPA national. Colliander brought a professional ALPA negotiator by the name of William McWilliams with him. McWilliams became the company's head of labor relations. Between them they worked to tear pilots' and mechanics' contracts apart. With Ruby just a friendly phone call away, Colliander focused on intimidating pilots into violating the contract and stretching FARs to the limit. As a New York Council representative, I heard the cries for help from pilots on a daily basis. Colliander's ploy was working and the company was making a mockery of our union.

One bitter cold winter day, on the last leg of a trip originating in Albany, I had a cold and felt like shit. There was delay after delay so that we were hours late arriving at Newark. At that time, Newark was a separate base from New York, which was the combination of LaGuardia and Kennedy. The schedule called for us to return by limo to the airport where we had parked our cars, whichever one it was.

The aircraft we brought in had a maintenance item on arrival that would take a couple of hours or more to fix. The crew scheduler in Utica thought it would be peachy if we stuck around and ferried the aircraft to one of the New York airports. I nicely told him that we'd already been on duty for about fourteen hours and Newark was a crew base; they contractually were required to call out a Newark reserve crew.

First thing you know, I get a call from Colliander, who was at home. He tells me that, contract or no, he is ordering me to wait for the aircraft to be fixed and then ferry it. I suggested he do the anatomically impossible and was fired for the third time. He later claimed his wife was insulted.

Unlike the run-ins with Jones, this was a much more serious situation. On the MEC, guys like Bernie Krouk and Larry Smith were very helpful. Nino Ciancetta and the regional ALPA VP were also extremely supportive. Nino was a Mohawk captain based in Boston and also regional safety chairman. Of course I immediately filed a grievance, but our expectations of Charley Ruby were not great.

To counter the company's pressure tactics, we immediately launched a pilots' work-to-rule campaign. In particular, we encouraged the pilots to write up elevator trim and control irregularities that occurred on the FH-227. There were also substantial briefings on other safety issues and the pilots' contract. Through the ALPA engineering department in Washington, we began to gather certification data on the FH-227 as well. The support from the pilots was fantastic.

After about a month and a half, the company and the MEC reached an accommodation, and I withdrew my grievance and was reinstated with pay. Not a fun time, but the blatant intimidation of pilots stopped. Unfortunately, not too long after the Colliander incident the company shifted its attention to the International Association of Machinists (IAM), the mechanic's union. As the reciprocating engines were being phased out by the BAC-111 and FH-227, management seemed to think mechanics were no longer as necessary as in the past—just fuel her up and go. After protracted negotiations under the Railway Labor Act (RLA), the mechanics went out on strike.

Also under the RLA, the pilots' contract remained in effect and we had to cross the IAM picket lines. The Mohawk MEC resolved that we would continue to fly so long as only a supervisory licensed mechanic then employed by the airline maintained the aircraft. No contract maintenance and no scabs. It was a sorry time that went on for months.

Bob Peach even had the balls to give the pilots a Christmas turkey as a bonus. At our suggestion, the pilots gave them to the mechanics walking the line.

Over time, the supervisory mechanics wound down like an old clock and it seemed an agreement between the IAM and the company was in sight. On cue, as if in a bad script, Bernie Krouk got a call from the United Auto Workers at the Fairchild plant in Hagerstown saying that an aircraft that they maintained was going to be ferried to LaGuardia the next day and be put back in service. That would violate the conditions the MEC had resolved for our continued service.

By that time Bernie was master chairman and I was New York Council chairman. I managed to bid the first trip to be flown out of LaGuardia and Bernie got the telephone hotlines burning. If confrontation was what the company wanted, we would be ready.

The truth is I always was a highly conscientious pilot who knew the equipment well. It was a good thing that evening at LaGuardia, because that damn airplane was a cherry. But no machine is flawless and I found the flaws. From dispatch to maintenance supervisors, I went through just about every VP with the company. Finally, after quite a while, I just couldn't find anything else and we set sail for Albany.

On the way to Albany, I noticed that the crew oxygen bottle seemed to have lost pressure. I conscientiously wrote it up and advised the mechanic supervisor at Albany that it would have to be repaired before we could go on. I was summoned to the phone again. This time it was Bob Peach roaring at me that I was fired and a few other things best forgotten. I think I got back to New York by Greyhound bus, all the time in touch with Bernie Krouk.

By the next morning, a widespread illness had infected just about every pilot scheduled to fly. It was an omen. And it did turn out to be a day of miracles. Within hours, the IAM had a contract and Bernie and I had caught a flight to Utica to meet with Peach. The meeting was over martinis in Peach's office and the dispute was all over, thank God. I thought of those cocktails just a few years later and felt that I could do business with Bob Peach. Unfortunately, it was never to be.

****

I wouldn't get a bid on the BAC-111 until 1969 and even then it was only as reserve captain at a small One Eleven base the company had established at Syracuse. After a few months of sitting around the Syracuse Airport Motel hoping for an occasional trip, I got a bid in Boston and would never be based in New York again. Most of the remainder of my career I spent as a commuter.

Mohawk Airlines BAC1-11 arriving at the gate on a snowy day at
Pittsburgh International Airport, PA.

Photo by Bob Garrard

When the company got the One Elevens and Fairchilds, it built a
modern training center with lots of glass at the Utica Airport, along
with a motel across the road that accommodated both company and
contract students. The heart of the training center was the One Eleven
and Fairchild simulators. It was state-of-the-art stuff and the training
that developed was excellent, a far cry from Wally Ott spending half
a day teaching us the DC-3. That period of time was the apogee
of the airline. Had labor/management relations been nurtured, the
future of Mohawk might have turned out differently. Who knows?
In the end, the government may wind up running all the airlines
anyway, in a never-ending circle of screw-ups.

At that stage in the development of simulator training, visual
simulation was primitive and some air work and takeoff and landings
were required in the aircraft. That is not so today. The whole shebang
is done in the simulator and the first actual ride in the aircraft is on
a scheduled flight with a line instructor/check pilot. When I checked
out in the B-767, it was the first time I physically set foot in the
airplane and I had a full ship going to Frankfurt.

The company did eventually figure out that its best instructors and check pilots came from the line and we had some that were outstanding. John Evans was my instructor for most of the simulator training and he was super. He didn't only train for the check ride— he taught you what you needed to know beyond the curriculum to lead a long life.

Training costs lots of money and while it is one of the costs of doing business, it is also understandable that airlines want to spend as little as possible. As a union rep, I always thought that professionally it was better for us to relax training pay and work rules to a fair extent, in exchange for longer and more comprehensive training. It was our careers and our lives that were on the line.

The traveling public should also be aware that cut-rate fares are not in their best interest if the airline has to cut training costs to the bone to compete. For a nation hooked on government sponsored gambling, do passengers really want to play air-chance at the ticket counter too?

You'd think that with training being a major expense the industry would want to retain its pilots as long as possible, wouldn't you? Wrong. Along with ALPA and the Allied Pilots Association (APA American), the industry supports forcing healthy pilots to retire at age 60.

I was a founder of the Professional Pilots Federation (PPF) in 1991. Its sole mission was to eliminate the FAA's age-60 rule, which forces airline pilots from the cockpit at that relatively young age. Airlines spend hundreds of thousands of dollars training pilots during their careers and then force perfectly healthy human beings to retire in what for many is the prime of life. In my long service, I had the benefit of a million dollars worth of training. The rest of the airline world has slowly changed its regulations, often fashioned after ours, to allow pilots to work longer. But this country has not. Stupidly, the United States has refused to budge, civil rights be damned.

I did the BAC-111 aircraft training out of Newark one night with my classmate, Arnie Atkatz. We ran up to Bangor to do approaches and what not. Arnie was a really good instructor who died much too young by his own hand in 1998. He had got into trouble with the IRS, retired early, and was eventually incarcerated and had his fishing boat confiscated in the Caribbean. A poor end for a good stick.

Marblehead Memories

Boston was a well-established large Mohawk base with John Wholley as the chief pilot. I got to fly quite a bit as a One Eleven reserve captain, but I still needed a place to stay. Reserve pilots were required to be able to report to the airport within an hour any time of the day or night and I sure couldn't do that from Long Beach. Bud Dean, who had flown with me in New York, had separated from his wife on Long Island and had an apartment in Marblehead. He was also flying out of Boston. I offered to split the rent on the Washington Street apartment and we had a deal.

Bud had a live-in girlfriend, Debby, who was a flight attendant with the company. I slept on the foldout couch in the living room and they had the bedroom. With our multiple flight schedules we were rarely all there at the same time. I went home to Long Beach on my days off and whenever else possible, in any case. But we still had a good time together. Bud has a terrific sense of humor and is one of the brightest men I've ever known.

Our apartment was one of five in a three story all wooden building, two to the first two floors and one larger one above. We shared the second floor with Dee, who lived alone. A flight attendant from another airline lived above. Her name is long forgotten, although I do remember that she favored leopard loungewear and funny cigarettes.

The same landlord owned a similar apartment building next door and we shared a parking lot, sort of a courtyard. Across Washington Street was Jake's Restaurant and bar, which served great flash grilled steaks and had a nice salad bar. Both bars were used frequently. My future wife, Sue, lived in a small house next to Jake's but we didn't meet until years later.

This was before the great real-estate boom that turned Marblehead into yuppie ville, back when the town was known for sailing and for its harbor, which is indeed beautiful. If those of us back then had had half a brain, we would have bought all the old houses in sight, but hindsight isn't worth much. I did eventually own two rental properties that did quite well. In any case, it was a nice place to live and there was a lot to do.

Up from the town wharf was another world-renowned bar and restaurant called Maddies Sail Loft. It was small and usually packed shoulder-to-shoulder in the narrow bar, but they offered huge drinks and the restaurant put up wonderful lobster.

On the water next to the wharf was the Drift Wood Restaurant. It wasn't much to look at but it was the place to go for breakfast. There were other places as well that made Marblehead fun.

Among his many talents, Bud was an excellent tennis player. I had never played before and would never be a challenge to him, but I did get better at ducking the ball. I enjoyed playing, though, and grew to a level where the game was fun.

Bud also had an eye for good buys. He found an old wooden dory for a song. We named it the Titanic. It needed two people to use, however, one to row like hell when the little hard-to-start engine quit and the other to bail. The boat wasn't exactly all that watertight. It eventually sank. The thing was, you didn't have to get far out to catch fish. Huge cod could be had just a few hundred feet from shore, along with striped bass, blue fish and other species.

After the sinking of the Titanic, I was prompted to try my hand at surfcasting. I got a long fiberglass rod and reel, the lures and all the other tackle. One summer evening, after a few martinis, I told Bud he could join me in going to the beach to catch our dinner. The wind was blowing in from the ocean and a light rain had begun. I assured him that was not a problem for someone with my skills. I put on my lucky lure and cast it out with all my might. The wind took it and returned it not ten feet from shore, where a nice sized striper gobbled it up as if sent by central casting! I reeled it in, modestly explaining how simple it was for those of us with talent, and we took our supper home.

****

After a while the girl with the leopard skin underwear moved out and Bud and Debby moved upstairs to the bigger apartment. In the meantime, I'd met Marilyn, a flight attendant, and fallen in love. It was a confusing time for me. I loved my wife and children, yet there Marilyn was. She knew I wasn't going to leave my wife and she saw other men. Sometimes she would fly with me and occasionally stay at the apartment. But I wasn't there on days off and when Bud and Debby moved upstairs I took another roommate, Peter Carpentier.

I met Peter through one of the pilots who used to fly with me, Rod Neibauer. Rod and his family had a nice home on the coast in Marblehead and I'd had dinner with them a few times. He was also the commander of a squadron in the Naval Reserve. Peter was a pilot in his unit. He was a lawyer by profession and at one time had studied to be a Catholic priest. As roommates, that gave us plenty to philosophize about. Fortunately, as a lawyer Peter worked mostly on financial stuff. I teased him that as a criminal defense attorney, with his Catholic sense of guilt, he'd be lucky to get me off with life for a speeding ticket!

Tragically, Rod's wife, who suffered from deep depression for years, took her own life in their Marblehead home not too long after I met Peter. Rod now lives in Florida and we still keep in touch.

Bud and Debby went on to get married and own a spectacular house with a swimming pool and tennis court in a beautiful part of Marblehead. Around that home formed a group that I didn't fit into comfortably, so I didn't see that much of them. Unfortunately, they separated and divorced. Apparently, Debby didn't get along too well with that group either.

Many years later, Bud retired early following a hard landing incident in a DC-9. He had waited too long to take control from the first officer and the landing badly damaged the aircraft. I spoke to him afterward and said he should be thankful no one was hurt, that shit happens and to forget it. His comment was, it happened on my watch. Bright people have a hard time forgiving themselves. I haven't seen Bud in many years, but I expect someday we'll have another martini together.

Marilyn would eventually dump me for a marriage prospect and so would my wife later on. My wife had been seeing someone for quite some time. I had suspected that, but knew for sure when a process server knocked on our Long Beach door and handed me the divorce petition. I'd gone through a period of my life that still gives me nightmares but, given the chance, I would do absolutely nothing differently. The formal separation by then was a relief. I had begun to feel like Alec Guinness in his classic role as a ferryboat captain between France and England who had a wife in both ports.

Sometime after Marilyn was history, Audrey, a neighbor in the adjoining apartment building whom I'd only known casually, called. She had just experienced a terrible tragedy and wanted to talk. I learned that she had been dating John Crumblish, one of our captains whom I had known well in New York. John was into acrobatic flying and lost a leg in a crash while performing. As a union rep, I helped him to regain his Class I Medical Certificate using a prosthesis, one of the first pilots in the country to do so.

Audrey had just returned from Hyannis on Cape Cod where earlier that morning, while performing in an air show, John had crashed his P-51 just a few hundred feet in front her. He was killed instantly. She was devastated. I was not only shocked but also pissed off. It was a lot of work getting him that medical certificate back!

Audrey was tall, slender and fashion model beautiful and for a short time we became friends and lovers. She suffered from MS symptoms that debilitated her from time to time and kept her at home. With my family responsibilities no less than before Marilyn left, I had little to offer when she also found a marriage opportunity. I don't know how that worked out for Audrey, but in my mind's eye she'll always be young and beautiful.

I had bought a nice rental duplex as an investment that in the tax environment of the day was doing well. That success prompted Peter and me to buy a large two family house on Prospect Street, up and around the corner from Shube's Market and Liquor Store. The plan was for him to totally renovate and live on the first floor and for me to do the same on the second. It was an old place that had been built upon, layer after layer. We thought the basement was the original structure going back to a pre-Revolutionary War grant from the king.

One St. Patrick's Day, Peter invited me to join him as a guest at someone's party. Mind, I don't think anyone had invited him but I didn't know that. That's when I met Sue. She told me later that she and her friends knew about the pilots across the street and didn't think much of them. I called her several weeks later. Over time one thing led to another and my life as Alec Guinness resumed. Sue was divorced and had a son, Griffin, who was about the same age as my youngest daughter.

Sue is extremely artistic and at the time taught pottery. She helped design the upstairs renovation and, having surrendered her Washington Street rented house, lived in the midst of the construction for months. We also set up a studio in the basement where she taught classes called the Backdoor Workshop.

We painted the house bright orange. It was easy to find and drew some comments from the neighbors, but most were favorable. It was an uplifting color and matched the St. Patrick's Day flag Sue made and thought appropriate to fly on that holiday. We got a Belington terrier we named Winston (after Winston Churchill, one of my heroes). Winston took Sue with him to pick me up at the airport.

Personal stuff, sure. I considered not sharing any of it. Yet, how could this be an honest and true story if I avoid a large portion of what shaped my life? I am neither a casual man nor an incapable one. My life is the result of deliberate decisions that for better or worse were mine.

I've known men who never cheated on their wives and have been married half a dozen times. And I've known others who would screw a snake if somebody held it. We all have known marriages held together by a convenience that shares far more animosity than love. Because a lot of my experience was painful, I became a student, read a lot and certainly thought a lot about marriage, both in our society and other's. Sue and I have had the benefit of some wonderful professional counseling.

After it all, I have come to the conclusion that caring for and loving another human being can never really be wrong if you behave responsibly. That the old "American" fantasy of boy meets girl in high school, are virgins when they marry, have a boy for her and girl for him and live happily ever after is, on the whole, a grievous flight from reality. I'm also convinced that most of humankind outside of America does not wish to imitate our concept of marriage. A good portion of the world, intelligently, if sometimes quietly, accepts extramarital relationships and/or practices polygamy. Many of those people think of us as being preoccupied with sex and adolescent in our social behavior.

Frankly, I get sick when I hear politicians sanctify marriage and the American family, when I know full well that all they're doing is passing the buck for their own lack of social responsibility. These same national heroes would be the first to foreclose on a woman's right of choice, as well as health care and education. I'm not belittling the need for marriage and stable families. Men and women and certainly their children need that. Yet divorce and loneliness are pandemic in America. Maybe we could do better if we were willing to look outside the box.

Sue and I have been together for more than twenty years. The Rev. Brendan Hadash, a Unitarian Universalist minister, married us at our home in Littleton, New Hampshire on August 31, 1985. My daughters and Sue's son Griffin were there, along with family, friends and neighbors. Sue's brother Bill has a wonderful voice and sang "Amazing Grace." I lost it and cried.

Striking Mohawk Down

Flying the One Eleven on Mohawk's short hops was challenging. Our pilots' contract followed the precedent set at American in reducing the monthly maximum flight hours from the 85 set by the FAA to 75 hours. When Allegheny got the DC-9s, they didn't follow that example and by continuing to fly 85 hours a month the pilots had an annual income that was among the highest in the industry.

When I started in 1959, Mohawk had no duty rigs to guarantee a ratio of flight pay hours to on-duty hours or hours away from base. I remember being stranded at the Airway Motel in Buffalo for several days because of a snowstorm. We were paid nothing and reimbursed something like 25 cents an hour for meals.

The first duty rigs at the Hawk guaranteed one flight pay hour for every four hours away from base and one flight pay hour for every three actually on duty. The pay for a trip was the greater of the two computations upon return to base. To earn 85 hours of pay a month could take as many as 340 hours away from base. That is twice as many hours as a 40-hour-a-week worker spends on the job.

That situation improved as tighter duty rigs were negotiated and computer programs came on the scene capable of juggling the airline's scheduled flights into trips for the flight crews. The trouble now is that the computers are superb at protecting the airline's purse and rotten at assuring that crewmembers are getting enough rest.

Unlike trunk line or overseas flights, our local runs rarely had a "cruise" portion and were more like missile projections. In high-density areas, and/or in bad weather, the cockpit workload could be intense. Increasingly, the role of the first officer became more important and captains had to create a communicative team to be successful.

A BAC-111 accident Mohawk had at Rochester brought the changing responsibility of a first officer to center stage in the industry. On a perfectly clear day, landing on runway 28 (which was adequate but not long for a One Eleven) the captain crossed the fence about 40 knots too fast and overran the runway. There were no fatalities, some minor injuries, and the aircraft was seriously damaged.

What the accident investigators and the FAA focused on was the lack of warning or communication from the first officer. He just sat there and let it happen. Now, anyone who has seen *The Caine Mutiny* with James Cagney knows that to take command from the captain of a ship is a deeply serious matter and can be considered mutiny. The same is true on an aircraft. But what if the first officer on a ship or aircraft sits there and permits an accident to occur while saying nothing? Is he culpable?

The FAA ruled yes and both the captain and first officer were penalized. In a careful analysis, the FAA maintained that the first officer's failure to alert the captain and break his fixation was a dereliction of duty. It was a landmark decision because there have been other accidents that might easily have been avoided if the first officer had spoken up.

Speaking up and actually taking command are different things. If the first officer had clearly advised the captain that he was way over the proper reference speed, he would have fulfilled his responsibility. The captain could have abandoned the approach and gone around. Or he might have responded in at least two other ways: "I see something that requires a higher airspeed; I have a reason." Or, "Shut up, kid, I'm the boss here."

The company laid out a more definitive policy to protect the first officer from retribution in reporting a captain, or refusing to continue a trip with a captain, who engaged in a nonstandard operation. Some years later that policy was expanded to a "two communication" standard. It is a method to identify a captain who has been incapacitated. It goes like this: "Captain, you're below the glide path." No response. Louder: "Captain, you're way below the glide path." If there is no response again, the first officer, with the help of another flight crewmember if available, is expected to take control and relieve the captain of command. It has happened and thank God the system works.

Flight crew communication is essential. The guys I hated to fly with, and there have been only a few, are those who got quiet and confused after saying "good morning." If he couldn't tell me that his wife was being a shit or the dog ate the cat, how is he going to get out, "Jerry that doesn't look right to me." It takes practice to communicate.

Anyway, I flew the One Eleven for several thousand hours from 1969 until a couple of years or so after Mohawk merged into Allegheny in 1972. Apart from the tragic accident in 1967 with Charley Bullock, the BAC-111 performed well, with no other major accidents for us.

There were only a few noteworthy mechanical problems I encountered with the ship. The Spey was a good engine, but the accessories were weak. Once I had a fuel controller limit the power on one engine to little more than idle. But that was no big deal because we where close to our destination and landed there with the engine running happily at idle.

On another occasion, I had a high-pressure duct blow a hole in the stub wing between the engine and the fuselage. That engine I shut down because of the danger of hot gas doing damage. The One Eleven performs well on one engine and it was not a problem. I've forgotten where I landed, but after half a day the company got some mechanics out to us and they made a temporary fix so the ship could be ferried out. They just secured the duct so no hot gas escaped and covered the hole with speed tape. Speed tape is this wonderful, expensive stuff that will stick to anything and stay there no matter how fast you go.

Another time, taxiing in after landing at Rochester, we had a fire warning on an engine. We shut it down and discharged both bottles of extinguishing agent to it with no success. I thought it was a fault in the sensing system, but we had no way to be certain so I had the aircraft evacuated and ordered the fire department to roll, although no flames were visible even from the tower. I directed the flight attendants to use the main air stair and no one was injured. Nine times out ten, if you do the full-blown emergency evacuation by deploying the chutes, someone will get hurt.

****

On November 12, 1970, the Mohawk pilots went out on strike. The strike lasted until the beginning of April 1971, over four months. It was a dreadful, uncertain time, not only for the pilots but also for all the other workers.

I had seen it coming months earlier, but I couldn't find a way to avoid it. We had been in contract negotiations for more than a year and were still deadlocked on just about every issue. The company, true to form, had been taking hostages by firing pilots and doing everything in its power to screw itself. These things can become a game of who blinks first. It is a dangerous game. Unfortunately, we had game players on both sides. Colliander and McWilliams tried to parley their union knowledge into a big win. Yet, as everyone knows, if there is a big winner in negotiations it is because someone got shafted and all you've done is postpone the problem.

Just a few months before the strike there was an election for a new master chairman; Bernie Krouk had done enough and was stepping down. The Master Executive Council was divided between those of us who wanted to continue negotiations and apply pressure in other ways while on the job, and those who felt the only answer was to go on strike. Jack Mozian became the candidate of the young Turks and I the candidate of the more moderate group. I lost by one vote and that was that.

Within weeks it became clear that the MEC and the negotiating committee were simply running out the Railway Labor Act mandated clock to a strike ballot. I could not support it and resigned from the MEC. Once on strike, I walked the picket lines along with everyone else.

In the background was the hope that cash-strapped Mohawk would be bought/merged into Allegheny, which had been making quiet overtures. Allegheny wanted the Mohawk routes and under the control of the CAB and the RLA the employees would go with the routes.

This occurred as it became evident that Mohawk could only emerge from the strike essentially bankrupt. It was the end for Bob Peach when the Mohawk Board of Directors began serious negotiations with Les Barnes and Allegheny.

I was one of the first to be recalled after the strike, on April 7, 1971. The first couple of months were chaotic. Just getting the idled aircraft back up was a problem. I flew for a few weeks as first officer on the FH-227 until the One Elevens got back on the line. I actually got to fly a local FH-227 trip as F/O for my old buddy JB Jones. One of the stops was at Watertown, New York. There was a wet spring snowstorm and JB got himself all messed up trying to taxi in the wind on slippery taxiways. I did my best to help him. After the actual Allegheny merger in May of 1972, all of Mohawk's nonunion pilots were let go.

We were lucky, pure and simple. If I had been elected and successful in postponing or avoiding the strike, the crisis might never had occurred and the merger opportunity would have been lost. On the other hand, the airline could have simply failed and Les Barnes wait to pick up the pieces, rather than actually merging the companies. Who knows?

ALPA provided strike benefits of about $350 a month and we were able to draw unemployment insurance, but it didn't add up to a lot. We also qualified for federal food stamps. I felt then and now that when a union strikes a company it is the equivalent of war; there should not be any other options and the workers should feel strongly enough to rate the job as not worth having.

What saved us was a system that placed value on labor and promoted economic development without licensing big business to disregard the society. Without question, had the Mohawk strike happened after 1978 and deregulation, Mohawk would have died and probably not gotten more than two lines notice in The Wall Street Journal.

Under ALPA policy there is a procedure to merge pilots seniority lists. Policy or no, it was not unusual for the larger surviving airline to simply bully through top-end seniority and leave the losers to fight it out in court, usually unsuccessfully. Les Barnes wouldn't permit that to happen. He wasn't going to have Peach's brand of labor relations on his property. To their credit, the Allegheny pilots went along with it and the merged list that came out was extremely fair, if not perfect. Some of the former Mohawk pilots chewed on it for years, but I thought the Mohawk working committee did a great job and the agreement was fair. I was frozen from the DC-9 for a while, but still earned more money flying the One Eleven.

Les Barnes went to pilots' meetings, both to reassure them and to shine on them. I had never seen anything like it. I think the Allegheny pilots would have physically carried the airplanes on their heads for him. One story that became legend tells of a senior captain getting carried away on a charter flight to the Caribbean somewhere. He got into some heavy gambling and put up the aircraft for collateral! Most CEOs would have had him beheaded, but Barnes bailed him out.

Before the changeover, Allegheny had line pilots spend time at the Mohawk bases to provide indoctrination. Allegheny ran its operation quite a bit differently than the Hawk, which tried to micromanage every flight. At Allegheny, the captain was boss, period. If he canceled a flight, it was all done; if he wanted more fuel, there was no question, and if there was a mechanical problem it got fixed. He was never second-guessed and pressured.

Through the years I witnessed the company suffer some foolish captains' decisions, but its policy was that it would rather suffer a foolish decision than have an accident. The company was right.

The new Boston chief pilot was Moe Blaine, affectionately known as "the suit." Moe always wore a suit and tie, left the heavy lifting to his secretary and more than anything wanted no waves. He just expected his pilots to go out and do the job and did his best to insulate them from the rest. It was a winning strategy. Unfortunately, that left him with a lot of free time on his hands and he was a heavy smoker. He died of lung cancer in 1986 and was replaced by my old classmate, Bob Knapp. Moe was also receptive to an invitation to go out for a beer toward the end of the day. Returning from a trip, it wasn't all that unusual to take off your uniform jacket, put on a sport coat and do exactly that.

But old habits die hard and all the newfound bonhomie took some getting used to. On one early flight as Allegheny approaching Pittsburgh around dinnertime, I radioed ahead and requested the station to pick up some hamburgers for the crew. It was a short turnaround and we hadn't eaten. The reply was that they were shorthanded and couldn't do that. This was a common station response at the Hawk and I responded immediately to set up a delay, because the crew was going for dinner. Sure enough, we pulled up to the jet-way and an Allegheny captain came on board with his arms full of food. He introduced himself as Bob Smith and asked if this was okay: He had lobsters and steak and God knows what else. It was the company's procedure to provide meals at mealtimes and this was simply normal. Well, I felt about two inches tall for expecting the worst and expressed my thanks to him for setting me straight. Bob was a nice guy who unfortunately died young in 1993.

On an early line check with an Allegheny check airman the weather at Indianapolis was below landing limits and communications with the station were not great. I requested alternate airport weather and operations was slow to respond. I didn't think much of it and, after holding for a while, the weather improved to limits and we landed. After going into operations, the check airman proceeded to chew the operations agent up one side and down the other. The gist of the message was, "when a captain asks you for important information, you provide it now, not when you have time." I was a little embarrassed, but what the check airman did was for my benefit: At Allegheny, the captain was expected to be in charge.

Then there was an incident at Bradley Field, Connecticut early one cold winter morning. The United States had just moved to a system of inspecting passengers and securing airports and aircraft. At Bradley, Operations was at ground level of one finger, the main terminal in the middle of another finger, forming a U. The One Eleven for our flight was parked at the other finger.

After preparing the flight plan, I told the crew that I would meet them in the employees' cafeteria in the basement level of the main terminal after I started up the ship's Auxiliary Power Unit to pre-heat the aircraft. The crew went in through the ground level of the finger and I schlepped across the wide ramp area to the other finger and the aircraft. I started up the APU, parked my things, and then went to the gate where my aircraft was parked. The gate door was locked but on the other side was one of the security guards, who was ignoring me. I got his attention and motioned for him to open the door. He adamantly motioned me away. Now, I'm just in my uniform jacket, no coat, and I'm freezing my ass off and this guy is being a jerk. I showed him a middle finger in the Italian salute and beat it back through operations to the cafeteria.

I had just joined the crew and sat down to eat when up came two state troopers in plain clothes. They told me to come with them. I asked what it was all about and what they thought they were doing. An American Airlines captain rose from the table next to us and asked the same thing. The troopers arrested us both!

They took us to the state police office on an upper floor of the terminal. We both said we wouldn't speak to them without an attorney and one could see they were beginning to recognize that maybe this wasn't too bright. While we were sitting there, a couple of hundred passengers are out of luck. What can they charge us with, asking a question? Or me with trying to hijack the terminal? After a while they decided on disturbing the peace and turned us loose on our own recognizance to appear in court at a later date.

Both flights wound up leaving about an hour late. En route to our first stop, I got a patched through call from Harvey Thompson, the vice president of flying. He wanted to know if everything was okay, did I need anything or could he do anything? I told him everything was fine and that I had sent him my summons to appear in court in about six weeks.

I didn't hear a thing from him until about five weeks later, when I was in recurrent ground school. First thing one morning, Harvey sent a message for me to come to his office down the hall. I'd never met him before, nor had I met Joe Rahill, the Allegheny ALPA master chairman, who was with him.

Now, Harvey was a little man, but it was said that when he stood on his desk he got a lot bigger. He didn't stand on his desk, but his message about the court appearance was that he'd spoken to the Connecticut State Police and they would drop the charge if I would apologize to the security guard. I told Harvey no way, no how, and that if the company wouldn't provide counsel I'd take care of it myself.

The next morning at about the same time Harvey came into the class and asked me outside. He said he'd talked to Mr. Barnes and that the company would take care of it. A couple of days later I got a telephone call from Gene Taylor, the executive vice president. He said the state police had dropped the charge and would be pleased if I'd stop in on my next trip through Bradley so they could apologize to me. Wow, what a company to work for!

I did stop in at the state police on my next trip through Bradley and it was worth the visit. They said they had responded as they would for a fellow police officer, but they were finding that the airline rent-a-cops were far from that.

****

Hijacking and terrorism were an airline problem long before September 11, 2001. The problem went back into the 1960s. In the United States, we had flights hijacked to Cuba, sons attempting to blow up their mother for the insurance, and assorted other crazies. In other parts of the world, there had been plenty of political terrorism. Sadly, however, we are still not dealing with security in a practical fashion and the additional cost to a fragile airline industry is helping to kill it.

Captain John Harkin had a B-727 hijacked to Cuba. Flight attendant Ilene Macalister had a would-be hijacker shot dead behind her by a police sharpshooter as the hijacker held her at knife point in the doorway of a FH-227 on the ramp at White Plains, New York. I had two incidents in the early days, one funny the other tragic.

One evening down the glass-exposed finger out to our gate at Rochester came a guy wrapped in a white sheet and running like hell to catch our flight. I invited the gate agent to tell me about our new guest in the elegant clothing. He explained that the gentleman had been taken off an earlier flight and rushed to the hospital due to an allergic reaction to his clothing's dry cleaning residue. He was just trying to get home. Okay.

Then, on a nighttime approach to Boston in a One Eleven, my flight became a factor in an unfolding drama. Some wacko had

101

broken into the cockpit of an Eastern DC-9, shot and killed the first officer and badly wounded the captain before the captain killed him with a crash ax. The captain was on the Boston tower frequency and instructed to land behind us on runway 22L. I abandoned the approach and told the tower we'd just go hold until he was down safely. We learned later that he was barely conscious from blood loss when the emergency medics arrived after the plane landed. The empathy I felt for him and his situation brings tears to my eyes to this day, almost forty years later.

Deregulation Blues

The 1970s, my second decade as an airline pilot, were chock-full of events. After the Mohawk-Allegheny merger, there was the Arab Oil embargo of 1973-74, which quadrupled the cost of petroleum and jet fuel. For a while it looked like the jet age would run dry. Then the Airline Deregulation Act of 1978 turned the industry upside down.

At the beginning of 1973, Richard Nixon was president and the U.S. Consumer Price Index was rising at a whopping 8.5 percent. Later in the year, on October 6, 1973, the Jewish holy day of Yom Kippur, Egypt attacked Israel across the Suez Canal at the same time Syria attacked on the Golan Heights. Just days before the war started, I was in Northern Israel at a kibbutz outside of Haifa with Carol and the children. We were visiting her uncle Pascah and his family.

During the two weeks we were there, Pascah had driven us all around the Golan Heights, where many of the tank battles would soon take place. Even then it was strange to see all the land mine signs along the roads and hear artillery thundering in the distance. Pascah said they were the good guys. I said I hoped so, because they were close.

Israel won the war big time and by November there was a cease-fire. In the meantime, on October 17, in support of Egypt and Syria, OPEC turned off the oil spigot on the West. By January 1974, the price of a barrel of oil rose from $3 to $11.65 in the United States.

Also, that prior November Congress had initiated the Trans-Alaskan oil pipeline. It was completed in 1977. The oil embargo was lifted on March 18, 1974, but the damage had been done. Between October 17, 1973 and December 6, 1974, the Dow Jones dropped 45 percent.

Sound familiar? Midway through 2003 the Dow Jones had dropped 40 percent in the last two years, Israel was under a constant terrorist threat as was the United States and the West, and the price of oil was skyrocketing because of the war with Iraq.

What was different for the airline industry is that back in the early 1970s the Civil Aeronautics Board regulated airline pricing and all of the airlines were able to raise prices collectively to cover costs without being accused of price fixing under antitrust laws. But by 2003 there was one big difference for the airlines. They had been deregulated since 1978 and raising prices collectively had become illegal. Major airlines were left to beg for government loans. US Airways and United Airlines were under the protection of chapter 11 bankruptcy, despite major labor concessions and tens of thousands of layoffs. The companies also brutally attacked pension plans, claiming loses created during the recession prevented them from honoring those contractual obligations.

How did it happen? Why did it happen? Whom do we have to thank for it?

It started when Senator Ted Kennedy held congressional hearings on deregulation in 1975. Alfred Kahn, a professor emeritus of political economy at Cornell University and chairman of the CAB, pushed hard for deregulation. He would also become an economic adviser to President Jimmy Carter, who signed the bill.

When Congress passed the United States Airline Deregulation Act of 1978, Chairman Kahn had convinced them that the act would produce increased service and cheaper fares. Congress had its head in the sand and Alfred Kahn stuck his where the sun doesn't shine! It was terrible legislation because major ramifications in an industry of extreme, unforeseeable variables were not considered.

Were there legitimate reasons to change the CAB regulatory system? Sure, but "high" prices was not one of them. Most of the price increases at the time had come from the oil embargo and were justified. The airlines also had to pay for the jet equipment that the public demanded and pick up the bill for an inadequate air traffic control system and deficient airports and, even then, for security.

What Congress needed to do was rejuvenate the good old boys' club that the CAB had become and be rid of Alfred Kahn. Weak management of protected major airlines needed to be prodded and competition introduced to improve overall service. Could we have conjured up an improved regulatory agency to either replace or improve the CAB? Of course, had Congress been willing to settle for a less than perfect solution, because there is no perfect solution. Kahn said the "free market system" was the answer. He was the chairman of the CAB and he should know best, right?

Wrong. Air transportation is a public service dependent upon too many factors to be completely turned over to the public sector. Since airline deregulation, we have seen similar fiascoes with communications and power deregulation. Kahn, the intelligentsia egghead, was a patsy for the free market mania that has expanded ever since, to the detriment of America and the rest of the world. Unfortunately, it took the poor fiscal policies of the Carter administration to open the door. I can't help but wonder what President Carter, a Nobel Prize winning humanitarian, thinks of the bill he signed now?

We know what Professor Kahn thinks; he still publishes papers lauding deregulation and the superiority of the free market system. He would deregulate the industry yet further by reducing the power the FAA inherited from the CAB and, perversely, he would vigorously enforce antitrust laws. Who does that leave standing? At least a laissez-faire government policy would do away with antitrust laws and leave one or two survivors. At the rate we're going, the federal government is going to be in the airline business because nobody else will be left.

Allegheny, freed by deregulation, expanded like crazy through the 1980s, buying Piedmont and PSA, changing its name to USAir and then to US Airways, at the time a close working relationship with British Airways was a possibility. But ultimately it ended up in Chapter 11 bankruptcy in August 2002 and again in September 2004, with a high probability that the airline would not survive. The FAA restrictions on U.S./foreign airline alliances prevented it from expanding a relationship with British Airways, and enforcement of antitrust laws by the Justice Department prevented it from merging with United Airlines or American Airlines. United Airlines followed US Airways into bankruptcy in December 2002 and is perhaps in even worse shape.

The combined US Airways/United Airlines would have been the largest in the world: 6,500 flights daily, 145,000 employees and annual revenue in excess of $25 billion. I find it hard to believe it would not have been a survivor. Was blocking it in the best interest of America or the world? I think not. It is just one of a growing number of governmental decisions driven by an extreme political ideology that ignores facts and renders us unable to cope with the demands of the 21st century..

My grandparents, Theresa and Philamino Manginello. Unfortunately she died well before I was born. I was very close to my Grandfather. He looked pretty much the same until the day he died.

My grandmother, Mary Sorlucco. We had dinner with her just about every Sunday—she would turn out fantastic meals from nothing. Her heart was a beautiful as her smiling face.

My parents, Jerry and Marie Sorlucco. I'm the
guy with the attitude. An only child and spoiled
rotten, I loved every minute of it.

Lou Mancuso, the owner and operator of Deer Park Airport. Lou always kept an eye on the operation and ran a tight ship.

Joe Paulsen, my first flight instructor. The first time he said, "you got it" and gave me the controls I was in seventh heaven.

Bill Ross, the fellow with the cap, was the flight instructor who soloed me. What a wonderful experience. I made three take-offs and landings— all the while singing the current Perry Cumo hit song, "Catch a Falling Start and Put it in your Pocket..."

Deer Park Airport Operation
building.

My friend Charley Giampa
cranking up a J-3; no electric
starters on those. Charley was
killed in an aircraft accident
that occurred near Idlewild
Airport shortly after this
picture was taken.

That's me. For weight
distribution the J-3 is flown
solo from the rear seat.
Instructors sit in the front.

Helen Mullen, Mother's oldest and closest friend—also a hot ticket in her day. She was my first passenger after I got a Private Pilots License on my 17th birthday.

This picture was taken shortly after I checked out as captain for Mohawk Airlines. I was 23 years old.

My wife Carol (long before we separated) , with our three daughters; left to right, Dana, Terry and Karen. The picture was taken on a trip to Gettysburg.

Irv Galley at the controls of a Martin 404. They didn't have auto-pilots—the aircraft was hand flown at all times. I learned a lot from Irv. He was definitely a good stick.

Sue's son Griffin, busting out of High School.

My wife Sue

Taking a break in the International Relief Officers seat over the North Atlantic on the return flight to Boston.

Dave Phipps, Sue and I on the tarmac in Frankfurt.

Ellie Zaleski, an old Mohawk buddy.

The crew in front of Olga's pub in Wiesbaden.

A crew shot after setting the brakes for the last time in Boston.

The Search for Safety

In 1975, the company broke the magic number of jets in service to satisfy the grandfather rights of former Allegheny pilots and I was able to move up to the DC-9. That same year Les Barnes left Allegheny to head Ryder Truck and Ed Colodny moved up to be president and chief executive officer of Allegheny. He'd been with the company since 1957 and had also worked for the CAB. He also, incidentally, strongly opposed deregulation.

We operated DC-9-30 aircraft and would later get some DC-9-50s and MD-80s with the acquisition of PSA. I never flew the MD-80; I instead transitioned to the B-727-200 in 1988. In thirteen years, I probably flew the DC-9 the better part of 10,000 hours. I really don't know precisely because I stopped keeping a logbook many years before. The diesel nine, as it was affectionately called, was a good, honest, straightforward aircraft and a workhorse for us. Bigger than the One Eleven, the DC-9-30 carried 110 passengers, three flight attendants and a flight crew of two. The lengthened -50 had room for 25 more passengers.

The -30 was powered by two Pratt & Whitney 14,500 horse power JT8D9 turbofans with a takeoff weight of 105,000 pounds. The -50 had P & W 15,500 horsepower JT8D15 engines with an increased takeoff weight of 121,000 pounds.

Unlike the One Eleven, the DC-9 had wing leading edge slats that allowed good slow speed performance and a better high altitude, high-speed wing when the slats were retracted. It handled a lot like a big fighter.

Allegheny Airlines DC9-31 at Pittsburgh International Airport.
Note: the United Caravelle in the background

Photo by Bob Garrard

In 1975, Allegheny's DC-9 simulator was housed in a cargo building at the Pittsburgh Airport. Primitive visual simulation was provided by optical projection to the windscreens from a camera directed by the simulator's computers. The simulation flew across a giant model landscape scene with an airport in the middle. It was like a giant full-wall model railroad with fake trees, houses and roads, the whole ten yards. If you crashed, the camera actually bunked into the model structures. It was really a hoot. A part of that model wall is displayed in US Airway's present training center. Modern state of the art visual simulation is now entirely computer generated and is excellent.

Each simulator training session is four hours long with a short break in the middle. The training department tried to pair a captain and first officer, but it was not unusual to have two captains go through the program together, in which case you would trade seats after the break, when it was the other student's turn. The whole program for initial equipment qualification was usually ten sessions, with the last being a rating ride by a FAA designated check airman. It is an intense couple of weeks, especially because everyone knows his (and now her) job is on the line. Some handle the pressure well, others don't. I always did pretty well, but I have great empathy for those that suffer from "checkitis." Remember the song that goes "don't worry - be happy"? Sure, but how about the mortgage, the kids in school and the fact that the profession you have trained a lifetime for is at risk every time you take a check ride?

The training department promoted the concept of "train like you fly and fly like you train." It means use standard procedures and standard phraseology all the time, not just for check rides. The concept works. I always operated by it and I always encouraged my students to do the same. It's like not lying, because it is easier not to have to remember what's standard, or the truth, and what is not.

Our instructor was Chris Ganas, an old hat in the training department. He was a colorful guy and a great instructor. Chris died in 2001. I've forgotten the name of my training partner. He was older than I was, pleasant to work with, but he had a little trouble with the program, particularly the V1 cuts.

The V1 cut drill creates an engine failure at or before V1 speed on takeoff. Prior to reaching that speed, there isn't sufficient control to keep the aircraft straight or sufficient power to successfully continue the takeoff and clear obstacles. The minimum control speed (Vmc) is a little slower than V1 but not much. The drill is usually simulated with restricted visibility, which requires an active instrument scan to keep from running off the runway. The danger of aborting the takeoff increases with speed and depends on the length of the runway. V1 for a particular takeoff weight would be the same for a 5,000-foot runway as for a 10,000 foot one. On the shorter one, an attempted abort after V1 might be impossible within the confines of the runway; on the longer, it could be a valid decision even though the takeoff could be continued. An example would be an engine fire. Why take a burning engine aloft and hope to extinguish the fire when a safe stop is totally possible? It is not a knee jerk decision, but rather a precalculated aircraft/runway performance point. Training for it takes repetition and learning how to equate warnings with the risk of action. Simply, you have to think before you act.

For instance, a minor warning light as you start the takeoff roll might warrant an abort to check out the system. At higher speeds, the abort is riskier than a minor system failure. An abort just prior to V1 on a shoehorn runway takes a maximum effort stop—full antiskid braking and reverse thrust to a complete stop, and even at that the nose wheel might be in the dirt. In real life, the wheels and brakes would be cherry hot and the tires may blow. It is serious, dangerous stuff.

At slower speeds, an engine failure below Vmc speed creates asymmetrical thrust that will take the aircraft right off the runway if the remaining engine isn't brought right back to idle. Of course any instructor worth his salt will at that point collapse the undercarriage to get your attention!

At V1, the asymmetrical thrust is manageable, but only if you are alert and with close to maximum rudder input. As the aircraft is rotated, the goal is leave the ground and climb at V2 speed, which provides stall protection and will also second stage climb performance to clear obstacles. In a swept wing aircraft (the DC-9 has a substantial sweep), if as the aircraft lifts off and is allowed to yaw because of insufficient rudder input, the power side wing advances, producing more lift as the wing straightens in relation to the air flow, and the unpowered side wing retreats, producing less lift. The result is called a "Dutch roll" and can be impossible to recover from as the aircraft sashays from one side to the other until ultimately hitting the ground. Not a good thing for one's morale and it earns a down on a check ride.

Movement and crashes in the simulator are quite realistic. The whole cockpit cab is an exact replica of the aircraft (the instructor's panel is behind the pilots) and sits atop gimbaled control arms. Once the door is closed and locked, it is free from the building and controlled by the simulator's computers. All seat belts and shoulder harnesses are fastened just like in the airplane. And for good reason: Not strapped in you would get thrown around like a rag doll!

For a pilot, a simulator session can really be a workout; it's all real. On the other hand, I've seen the technicians climb into the seat and use the simulator like a laptop computer. The mindset is different. It is also true that, as good as they are, simulators are not airplanes. They are wonderful, safe procedures trainers, but not great for teaching airmanship. As an instructor, I often thought how wonderful it would be to have a little training jet available to go play and teach some basic airmanship. Unlike the early days, when wings fell off and engines were unreliable, today's equipment is excellent and most accidents are the result of pilot disorientation. These are avoidable.

****

While statistically most accidents are attributed to pilot error, not all are. Some are like the green hand of death reaching up for you.

On July 17, 1996, TWA flight 800, a B-747-100 blew up while climbing through 13,800 feet ten miles off the coast of Long Island after departing Kennedy en route to Paris, killing 249 passengers and the crew of 32. At first it was thought to be a bomb or a missile attack, but later the National Transportation Safety Board (NTSB) found it to be the result of faulty wiring to a fuel boast pump.

The fuel boast pump wiring problem was approached by increased maintenance inspections and by changing procedures. Hitherto, standard operating procedures were to burn a fuel tank dry before turning the electrical boast pumps off. Now SOP is never to have the pumps on in a dry tank. A faulty pump can explode a fuel/air mixture, but not liquid fuel.

The day after the TWA flight blew up, I had an interesting experience at Boston's Logan Airport before a flight to Frankfurt. In briefing the crew, I had talked about TWA and emphasized that we should be alert in regard to security. It was a through flight from Charlotte, North Carolina, with some passengers continuing on to Frankfurt. When I boarded the aircraft, my lead flight attendant, a very senior, sharp gal, told me we had a problem. One of the passengers from Charlotte who was supposed to go through abruptly got up and left the airplane. The agent was in the process of trying to find him. He had no luck. I went with the agent in search of both the passenger and the State Police officer who was supposed to be the muscle behind the unarmed security employees, but he was not to be found. We proceeded to treat it as a serious bomb threat. Everybody was taken off the aircraft and every piece of luggage was identified by its owner and hand searched.

The station did a great job. We left about 45 minutes late, but with favorable winds still arrived close to schedule. Was I surprised that the terrorists chose Logan as the launch point for all three airliner attacks on September 11, 2001? No, I wasn't. Logan security had been extremely weak for years. America was ripe for attack.

On September 12, 2001, only a day after 9/11, American Airlines flight 587, an Airbus 300-600, came apart after takeoff from New York's Kennedy Airport and crashed into Rockaway, killing 251 passengers and the crew of nine, as well as six others on the ground. With the smoke still rising from the World Trade Center, initial reaction was that it was another terrorist attack.

But, as the debris was recovered, there was no evidence of an in-flight explosion or missile strike. After a sizable portion of the vertical stabilizer was pulled up from Jamaica Bay, all eyes turned to the point of separation; it looked like it had been cut off with a pair shears. The National Transportation Safety Board later discovered that serious delamination of the composite skin of the vertical stabilizer had occurred.

The NTSB also learned from the flight data and voice recorders and a review of air traffic at the time of the accident that flight 587 had encountered wake turbulence just before the break up occurred, and that large rudder control inputs had resulted. The board further postulated that those inputs to a weakened structure could have been the straw that broke the camel's back.

That reminds me of the in-flight break up of a Lauda Air Boeing 767-300ER over Thailand on May 26, 1991, which killed 213 passengers and the crew of 10. The probable cause of the accident was found to be an uncommanded in-flight deployment of the left engine thrust reverse, which resulted in loss of flight path control. The incredible yaw, Dutch roll and aircraft overspeed destroyed the airplane. The Thailand Aircraft Accident Investigative Committee recommended that the FAA examine its certification philosophy in regard to safeguards for ground only engine thrust reverse systems.

Different mechanical or structural failures between the two accidents to be sure, but the traveling public should be aware that most of the FAA aircraft certification data is provided by the manufacturer and accepted as the word of God. The public should also know that the FAA mandate under law is both to provide air safety and to promote air commerce. Would you give that same conflicting mandate to your hometown fire marshal? I wouldn't.

On September 8, 1994, there was an accident that really struck close to home. USAir flight 427, a B-737-300, crashed on approach to runway 28R at Pittsburgh, killing 127 passengers and the crew of five. Leveling off at 6,000 feet at 190 knots, the aircraft entered the wake vortex of a Delta B-727 about four miles ahead. During the ensuing rock and roll there was an uncommanded full left rudder deflection. Remember the deadly Dutch roll? Well, after several other gyrations the aircraft rolled through inverted flight and crashed nose first into the ground.

Attention turned to another mysterious B-737 crash a few years earlier. On March 3, 1991, United Airlines flight 585, a B-737 crashed on approach to Colorado Springs in clear weather conditions. Witnesses reported the aircraft rolled steadily to the right and pitched down. The crew of five and 20 passengers were killed.

The NTSB determined the probable cause of both accidents was loss of control resulting from movement of the rudder to its blow-down limit opposite to that commanded by the pilot as a result of a jam of the main rudder power control unit servo valve. Not an exact quote, but close enough.

The USAir/ALPA accident committee did a tremendous amount of work trying to duplicate the circumstances of the accident, both in the aircraft and in the simulator. Consequently, the rudder control system has been updated and training procedures designed for the simulator on all the different types of aircraft to include semi-acrobatic recovery training.

This training to recover from extreme unusual attitudes is vital. Once the nose of a large aircraft gets straight down there is no recovery; the aircraft will either overspeed or G-forces will be exceeded in trying to pull out. Consequently, if for some reason the aircraft becomes inverted, the only recovery is to continue the roll. On my very last six-month simulator check, the instructor asked if there was anything I wanted to do. So I did a roll and attempted a loop. As expected, the 76 rolled like a top, but the loop couldn't be completed. I pulled too many Gs trying to come out the bottom and it was all over.

In the few accidents that I have rehearsed, 927 people lost their lives. In that same time frame, thousands more were killed in airline accidents around the world. They average about one a week, but don't usually get headline news coverage. They happen in Third World countries with old airplanes and inexperienced crews, right? Not always.

The air, like the sea, is very unforgiving and accidents will happen. The trick is to keep the odds overwhelmingly in favor of the house. Ultimately, the captain is constantly weighing those odds. The aircraft manufacturer, the government and airline management will deeply regret an accident but it's only the captain and crew who share your fate as a passenger. They sit in the point end, which gets there first.

Considering the stress the U.S. airline industry is undergoing, it is absolutely amazing that our accident rate has remained so low. I don't think it will continue that way if we don't bring economic sanity back to American aviation. The financial liability of accidents alone should be sufficient to impel the industry to stop attacking its pilots and other professionals. A new wide-body aircraft goes for over a hundred million dollars and personal liability can go for a million dollars a fatality. Throw in collateral damage and just one accident can cost three to four hundred million dollars easily.

The bean counters will say risk is one of the costs of doing business. Sure, but when a couple of major accidents can put an airline in the financial crapper, it should be weighed against the savings in raping labor. Unfortunately, the truth is that in America we have tolerated CEOs who are more interested in feathering their own nests than in the survival of the companies they run.

****

The advent of jets increased the demands on the airport environment and the Air Traffic Control system (ATC). While it is easy to think of the sky as infinitely big, it all boils down to the availability of runways, those finite strips of concrete. No matter if it is carrying two passengers or two hundred, that airplane owns the runway for the minute or so it takes to land or takeoff. That means a single runway can handle about 60 operations an hour, give or take a few. The world's major airports may be able to use three runways, usually dedicating one for takeoffs, one for landings and the third one swinging for either.

Airplanes can't pull alongside the road and stop while waiting for a place to land, so if there is too much traffic they have to enter a holding pattern. The standard pattern is a four minute left or right racetrack from a fix. Airspeeds are reduced to 200 knots indicated air speed (KIAS) 6,000 feet or below, 210 - 230 KIAS above 6,000 feet to 14,000 feet and 265 KIAS above. The stack of aircraft is separated by 1,000 feet, with flights normally taken off the bottom by the radar approach controller. Horizontal separation is a minimum of three miles. Thus there forms a procession of airplanes trailing to land. At busy times, that is a lot of metal over a small amount of real estate. The big sky can be full of airplanes and collision is a major specter.

One of the first jet airliner midair collisions happened over New York City on December 16, 1960. I remember shopping with Carol in downtown Utica when it came over the news and being concerned about my parents in Brooklyn, where some of the wreckage came down. It involved a United DC-8 from Chicago to Idlewild and a TWA Super Constellation from Dayton to LaGuardia. One hundred thirty-four passengers and crewmembers died and, amazingly, one child survived.

Investigators found that the DC-8 had barreled through the holding pattern it had been assigned because it was going too fast to stay within its confines. A jet doing 350 KIAS will cover (even at low altitude) six miles a minute. The accident caused a change in

Federal Air Regulations to reduce the speed of aircraft below 10,000 feet to below 250 KIAS, with no exceptions, along with additional restrictions on holding pattern airspeeds.

On July 19, 1967 a Piedmont 727 climbing away from Asheville, North Carolina airport hit a Cessna 310 about eight miles from the airport. All five crew members and 74 passengers were killed, as were the three occupants of the Cessna.

A couple of years before the Allegheny/Mohawk merger, on September 9, 1969, Allegheny flight 853, a DC-9-31, collided with a Piper Cherokee on approach to Indianapolis. Flight 853 was on an instrument approach just breaking out of the clouds at 3,000 feet. Although the DC-9 was on approach control radar, the Cherokee was not equipped with a transponder and the radar in use was unable to pick it up as a raw data target. The four crewmembers and 78 passengers were killed, as were the two occupants of the Cherokee. The captain was James Elrod and the first officer William Heckendorn.

Prior to the World Trade Center record of about 3,000 fatalities, the record in aviation was 582 killed in a runway collision at Tenerife, Canary Islands, on March 27, 1977. A KLM 747-200 with 249 on board misunderstood a takeoff clearance in fog and crashed into a Pan American 747-100 with 394 on board that was still on the runway after landing. The 61 survivors were on Pan Am. Interestingly, both flights had been scheduled to land at Las Palmas and were diverted because of a bomb explosion at the Las Palmas airport.

On September 25, 1978 a Pacific Southwest (PSA) 727-200 had a midair collision with a Cessna over San Diego. All seven crew members and 128 passengers on the 727 were killed, as were both occupants of the Cessna and 13 others on the ground.

On February 1, 1991 a USAir 737-300 at Los Angeles was cleared to land on a runway that a Skyway Metro III was on, holding for takeoff. The aircraft collided and burst into flames. Two of the six crewmembers and 20 of the 83 passengers on the 737 were killed, as were the two crewmembers and 10 passengers on the Metro.

Bottom line: Midair and ground collisions are a major hazard to aviation. Interestingly, most midair collisions have happened in good weather during daylight hours. The majority of ground collisions occur during low visibility and/or darkness.

The best safeguard is constant alertness to all traffic movement and an active outside scan. Cockpit workload and pilot discipline must always provide a pair of eyes to be looking outside in visual conditions. This was a big issue when the regional jets came. The argument came down to whether two pilots could provide safety, or should there be three? For the longest time United Airlines pilots insisted on a flight crew of three on the 737; others flying them did not. The third pilot on United 737s had absolutely no duties. All the DC-9 and One Eleven operators did so with two pilots.

Was it safe? Is it safe now? Yes and no. The aircraft cockpits were designed for two pilots and could be flown by one, if the other one was incapacitated. Technology then and now allows that. That said, I think we have pushed the envelope way too far. The largest aircraft now built, holding several hundred passengers, require only two pilots. The Boeing 767 I flew was one of the first big, wide bodies to allow that. In fact, Boeing didn't know if the FAA would allow a two pilot crew and at first provided a third pilot's station. What's being overlooked because of cost is the workload demanded to properly manage and service the cabin. The captain signs a flight release accepting responsibility the whole ship, not just the flight crew.

In a hotel, restaurant or big store, the management provides some emergency services and then calls for help. We don't have that ability in flight. If there is an event in the cabin, such as a fire or mechanical problem, say a lavatory gone berserk and overflowing, or even a medical emergency, sending one pilot back can create a tremendously high workload on the flight deck, with no backup. Add to that security concerns (the FAA is even allowing some pilots to carry guns) and it gets scary.

Doris Day did a great job in a movie of landing an airliner by being talked down, after the pilots were incapacitated. What do you think the odds really are for that happening? The answer is zero.

The cost of a third pilot on a large, wide-body aircraft that carries more than 200 passengers would be only a few dollars a seat, and if every airline was required to provide one it wouldn't be a competitive cost factor. With reasonable cooperation between the pilots unions, airline management and the FAA, the third pilot could function as a relief officer on flights over eight hours. If the industry were willing to break the paradigm, the third pilot would fit in and be a great asset to flight safety. I think the alternative is to increasingly isolate the flight deck crew from the passengers, much like an automated train. At that point my flight kit would likely contain a parachute!

As far as midair collision goes, the development of Traffic Collision Avoidance Systems (TCAS) has been a tremendous improvement. It is a fairly sophisticated system that requires a radar transponder on both aircraft and special instrumentation to work. The units interrogate one another to provide oral and visual traffic advisory (TA) information or, if a collision course is calculated, a resolution advisory (RA). The RA will indicate a fly up or down target arc on the vertical speed indicators. It doesn't call for a turn, just up or down.

It works but, since light aircraft are not required to have the equipment, eyeballs are still the first line of defense at low altitude. Flying the One Eleven and DC-9, unless we were in Instrument Meteorological Conditions, I insisted that a pair of eyes always be scanning the outside. Otherwise, it is so easy to find both pilots fiddling with the radios or doing other things. Since the risk obviously increases near airports and at low altitudes, USAir and its predecessors were particularly vulnerable and, as you have read, paid the price.

Ground collisions are still a tough nut. Large airports such as Los Angeles International, Kennedy, Chicago's O'Hare, Frankfurt, London and many others, can have hundreds of aircraft either parked at gates or remote hard stands or in motion. A lot of progress has been made with ground lighting and markings. At US Airways, we always taxied with the FO physically holding and tracking our progress on an airport ground chart. Taxiing a large aircraft is a hoot. The 76 is half a football field long and again as much from wing tip to wing tip, plus you sit about three stories high. Fortunately, all the large airports now have ground control radar, which has helped a lot, because when the visibility is down the control tower is usually up in the clouds.

****

The National Transportation Safety Board is an independent federal agency charged by Congress to investigate every civil aviation accident in the United States, as well as significant accidents in other modes of transportation. It determines the probable cause of the accident and issues recommendations to prevent future accidents.

Since its inception in 1967, the NTSB has investigated more than 114,000 aviation accidents and is considered one of the world's premier accident investigation agencies. Twenty-four hours a day, every day of the year, the NTSB has a team of investigators ready to launch to an accident site anywhere in the world.

Although the NTSB has no regulatory or enforcement power, its recommendations are followed about 80 percent of the time and have helped shape aviation safety. The FAA, airline management and aircraft manufacturers that on the whole are more concerned with covering their butts, regrettably juxtapose the NTSB's reputation for thoroughness and impartiality.

The Airline Pilots Association also has an accident investigation go-team ready at all times. It has done a great job in protecting the reputation of the pilots involved. Most times they are dead and can't speak for themselves when others pass the buck, claiming that only "pilot error" was responsible for the accident. In court, liability can cost hundreds of millions of dollars.

No pilot crashes on purpose unless it is a suicide. That has happened in little airplanes, just as it is known to happen frequently in cars. The only exception I know of is the Egyptian pilot who crashed an airliner into the sea a few years ago in an apparent suicide. As a young flight instructor, I came frighteningly close to being a victim of a suicide-murder. I had given a series of lessons to a middle-aged building contractor in his own Cessna 140. One summer day he wanted to buzz along the beach at Fire Island. It wasn't unusual to find naked girls sunbathing and, what the heck, I didn't mind that. So we went right down on the water and flew ten or fifteen feet along the beach. To my chagrin, everybody had clothes on.

The next day I was shocked to learn that my student had committed suicide by carbon monoxide poisoning in his garage. All it would have taken as we flew along the beach was a push on the control wheel and both our deaths would have been considered an accident. You never know what someone else is really thinking. In the end, this poor tormented soul could and did commit suicide, but apparently couldn't commit murder.

In my experience, accidents almost always have multiple contributing factors and simply to find the pilot culpable will not prevent the next accident. In that context, the term "pilot error" is much more complex.

When a pilot who is negligent, reckless, not proficient, or simply stupid is involved in an accident, it is because somewhere along the line his chief pilot was negligent for not firing his ass. Consequently, if you are interested in preventing a similar accident, you fix the airline's chain of command and supervision. The fool is likely dead anyway and is not going to do it again.

Pilots are human beings. Engineers hate them. Humans perform many tasks badly. We don't do well with repetition because we get bored. Our senses are weak and our brains are probably oversized. Most birds have better eyesight and any dog can outhear and outsmell us. Because pilots are also smart, they are given to outsmarting the engineers. Give an engineer a good machine any day! Except that humans have intuition and are smart enough to know fear. If I had to name an attribute I looked for most in a pilot, it would be the ability to deal with abstract thought.

In the early days, pilots flew in open cockpits. The idea of enclosing the cockpits scared them silly. They wouldn't be able to hear and feel the air. Until a flight instrument called a turn and bank indicator was invented, pilots couldn't fly without reference to a visual horizon. The pilot would confuse the G forces on his body and invariably enter a dead man's spiral. To be an instrument pilot, you have to learn to ignore your physical senses and totally trust the instruments.

Early biplanes flew slow and low. Today's are like guided missiles by comparison. There are no sensual feelings that are reliable. Flight is in an abstract environment, so the pilot must have constant spatial orientation. Consequently, most pilot error accidents are the result of the pilot losing spatial orientation and flying into the ground.

Beginning in the early 1970s, a number of studies looked at the high occurrence of "controlled flight into terrain" (CFIT) accidents, where the crew hits the ground or water with no apparent awareness, because crewmembers are spatially disorientated. These accidents were often associated with nonprecision instrument approaches or descent from high altitude in mountainous terrain. Mohawk's FH-227 accident at Glens Falls in 1969, during a Visual Omni Range approach, is an example.

Because of the recommendations of the NTSB, in 1974 the FAA required all Part 121 certificate holders, certified airlines, to install Ground Proximity Warning System (GPWS) equipment on turbine-powered aircraft. The thought was that the complexity of such aircraft created a higher disorientation factor for pilots. The FAA would lower the bar over the years to include aircraft in other segments of aviation.

Here are some of the more notable CFIT accidents:

* 1945: B-25 bomber crashed into the Empire State Building, killing 23.

* 1950: Vickers Viking crashed in the fog near London Airport, killing 28.

* 1951: United DC-6 crashed northwest of Denver, killing 50.

* 1956: Canadian airliner crashed into the mountains near British Columbia, killing 62.

* 1965: American Airlines B-727 crashed on approach during visual conditions, killing 58.

* 1966: TABSO Bulgarian Ilyushin-18 crashed into the mountains surrounding Bratislava, Czechoslovakia (now Slovakia) after takeoff, killing 82.

* 1971: Alaska Airlines B-727 crashed into Mount Fairweather while attempting an instrument landing at Juneau airport during a heavy snowstorm, killing 109.

* 1972: Eastern Airlines L-1011 Tristar crashed into the Florida Everglades 14 miles west of the Miami airport, killing 99 of the 176 on board. While circling at low altitude, the crew got preoccupied trying to trouble shoot an unsafe landing gear light problem and allowed the airplane to fly into the ground

on autopilot. This was a focus accident that caused the NTSB to recommend GPWS.

More recently, in a CFIT accident northeast of Cali, Colombia, on December 20, 1995, an American Airlines B-757 on approach crashed into the mountains, killing all 159 on board. Although the aircraft had GPWS, it did not provide ample warning time for the crew to avoid the mountainous terrain. As a result, the NTSB recommended enhanced GPWS that had the ability to look further ahead.

The GPWS system on the 76 gave alerts when one of the following thresholds is exceeded below 2,450 feet radio altitude:

Mode 1 - Excessive descent rate.

Mode 2 - Excessive terrain closure rate.

Mode 3 - Altitude loss after takeoff or go-around.

Mode 4 - Unsafe terrain clearance while not in the landing configuration.

Mode 5 - Below glideslope deviation.

Windshear Mode - Significant windshear exists.

The system would yell at you "whoop whoop terrain" and red warning lights would flash. The drill was to pull up immediately.

It was an excellent system that perhaps has been updated since I flew the aircraft. There was talk of linking it to global positioning (satellite) so that ultimately there could be full-time terrain mapping.

In the end, spatial orientation in every realm of flight is the goal. Because any pilot can lose the big picture, crew coordination and standard operating procedures are every airline's training mission. Instructors and check airmen know that regardless of warning devices a disorientated crew is an accident in progress.

Because of NTSB recommendations, two other big accident generators, wind shear and runway overruns, have been greatly reduced. Between the two, thousands have perished.

One type of wind shear can be thought of as a fast moving river's relationship to the shore: An object moving from one to the other will experience either rapid acceleration (increase in performance) or deceleration (decreased performance). The other type is downbursts, which are strong downdrafts that induce an outburst of damaging winds on or near the ground. Weather phenomena that cause wind shear are jet streams, high gradient frontal activity, and convective weather, which includes thunderstorms, tornadoes and microbursts.

Shear encounters with jet streams are at high altitude and high speed and are generally called clear air turbulence. They can be very severe and have caused major upsets resulting in airframe damage and fatalities. Weather radar can't pick them up because there are no water droplets in the air to provide a Doppler effect. Our best information is from pilot reports from preceding flights along the route and by observing rapid changes in outside air temperature.

Tornadoes only exist imbedded in thunderstorms and thunderstorms, with or without a funnel core, have a deadly history in aviation. Early weather radar helped but had tremendous limitation and was a lot like interpreting an X-ray. The invention of Doppler computer enhanced in color radar was a great improvement. The speed and altitude that jets operate at en route also enable detours of hundreds of miles around lines of thunderstorms and the airplanes are above a lot of the weather. Unfortunately, many of those advantages vanish in airport terminal areas.

Shears can and have been real killers during takeoff and landing in rapidly changing wind conditions. Here are just a few notable fatal accidents attributed to wind shear:

* 1975: Eastern B-727 crashed landed short on Rockaway Boulevard on approach to JFK, killing 113.

* 1985: Delta Lockheed Tristar crashed on approach to Dallas airport, killing 134.

* 1994: USAir DC-9 crashed attempting a go-around at Charlotte, North Carolina, killing 37.

Wind shear is dangerous on both takeoff and landing because of the small margin of airspeed above stall and the close proximity to the ground. We trained crews to execute recommended recovery procedures immediately if a deviation from any of the following occurred:

Takeoff: + or - 15 knots indicated airspeed

+ or - 500 feet per minute vertical speed

+ or - 5 degrees pitch attitude

Approach: + or - 15 knots indicated airspeed

+ or - 500 feed per minute vertical speed

+ or - 5 degrees pitch attitude

+ or - 1 dot glideslope displacement

Unusual throttle position for a significant time.

Recovery is not for wimps. It is balls-to-the-wall power and increased pitch attitude to a target of 15 degrees. In a severe downdraft or deceleration in airspeed, we considered it acceptable to hold pitch even if the stall warning came on intermittently. Even that maximum effort can fail and the aircraft strike the ground. The answer is to avoid, avoid and avoid!

Because the FAA and the industry have followed NTSB recommendations, we are now able to forecast and detect terminal area wind shear much better by surrounding the airport terminal area with Doppler radar and real time wind observations. Crew training in the simulator has made pilots better able to recognize wind shear immediately and save precious seconds to recover.

****

Throughout the history of aviation, runway overruns have happened a lot. Think of a heavy ten wheeler construction truck loaded to the gunnels to a weight of a hundred thousand pounds trying to stop on a wet or icy road going at 150 miles per hour, then imagine the distance it would take to stop. That is equivalent to a small DC-9, which has only four braking wheels, not ten.

All jets have anti-skid braking that has improved over the years. The earlier systems would lock a wheel on occasion, resulting in an immediate blowout. The trick is to keep the wheels turning and transferring braking friction into heat. If water is standing on the runway, the tires will stop rotating and hydroplane on a pocket of steam resulting in no braking at all and you're screwed. Hydroplaning accidents happened a lot, some with fatal results.

Airliners have the additional braking available of reverse thrust, although it is not used to set runway length criteria. Military fighters and other types don't have reverse but deploy drag chutes to help stop. Military airports also employ runway end barriers that are not used at civilian airports. Safe extensions of runways for undershoot and overrun protection are a luxury most civilian airports don't have. It is not unusual to have a runway end at a gully, cliff, road or other obstacle.

The problem was how to get rid of the water on the runways. Deep treaded tires, such as all-weather automobile tires, cannot sustain the high speeds required by an aircraft. They fly apart. The answer was to carve the tread into the runway instead, by grooving across its entire length. That gives the water a way to escape from beneath the tire. It works. Overrun accidents have gone down dramatically.

None of the technology and none of the advances made in air transportation has come cheaply, neither in lives nor in money. Air travel can be an excellent dollar value as a mode of transportation and it is essentially irreplaceable for long distance travel. But it cannot be a cut-rate mode of transportation without self-destructing. We are proving that now.

As we look ahead, larger, faster aircraft will have to venture higher in the stratosphere and perhaps long-range flights will even become suborbital. Does any thinking person believe that building such aircraft/spacecraft and the operating system capable of supporting them is going to happen in today's cutthroat economy? I sure don't.

At the same time, aping the apparent success of Southwest and a few of the cut-rate airlines that are managing to eke out a profit by a combination of using smaller aircraft, offering few passenger amenities and paying low wages, doesn't factor in the cost, needs and restrictions of the total air transportation system. Cut-rate airlines are sandbagging the industry and dragging it down.

The taxpayer is the ultimate chump. We pay for the nation's navigational aids, the Air Traffic Control system, airports, FAA, NTSB, security and the countless other things necessary to provide air transportation. Then we allow FAA certified air carriers to provide substandard service, with inefficient aircraft, only to the communities they wish to serve, while ignoring others. There seems to be no limit to the government's tolerance. We then stand aside as airline boards of directors defraud stockholders and pay exorbitant salaries and bonuses to managers, while attacking labor and its accrued benefits and pensions.

Since deregulation and the strangulation or demise of most of the nation's airlines, only 25 percent of the four hundred or so air carriers the FAA has certified are still in business, which means that 75 percent have failed! Most of the survivors are small commuters; no major national or international airline has emerged. After twenty-five years, it is time to move on, time for the federal government to consider its obligation to the American people and quit playing lackey to the big shots and special interests who have sucked the system dry.

Flying Was The Fun Part

I flew the DC-9 for thirteen years, from 1975 to 1988. As I said earlier, that was easily over 10,000 flight hours, which is probably as many as any pilot on the planet. It was good duty.

The cockpit was comfortable and roomy, at least to the back of the pilots' seats, which had a narrow passageway with a small closet on the right side and bulkhead on the left. In between, a jump seat could be folded out and locked in place, although it was not very comfortable. The front section was taken directly from the DC-8. The entry cockpit door folded in and had a lock and key, but a good kick would open it.

The main passenger entranceway was to the left behind the cockpit bulkhead and opposite, on the other side of the aircraft, was an emergency exit that was also used to service the adjacent galley. There was also a rear stair that, with the advent of jetways, was never used and eventually removed to save weight. Behind the rear cabin pressurized bulkhead, the door leading to that stairway was also used as an emergency exit. With the stair retracted or removed, a ramp led to the tail cone, which could be jettisoned. In that unpressurized area was the auxiliary power unit and its associated ducting and wiring. The rear pressure bulkhead would later be subject to fatigue that required major maintenance.

A typical flight would be from Syracuse to Newark and take about 50 minutes, most it going up and then down, entering landing

137

traffic. During that short time, the three flight attendants served beverages, cocktails and even hot meals in insulated trays to 105 passengers! The attendants were always climbing uphill or running downhill with the change in deck angles. A 25-degree bank, which is the minimum expected by Air Traffic Control, will pull slightly less than half a G, creating a weight increase of almost 50 percent. That 125-pound attendant would suddenly hit 180! They all wore support hose because of the danger of varicose veins. A pilot who got overzealous in a turn would be chided that he'd used six hours worth of their eighteen-hour bras.

Crank in some normal northeastern bad weather and turbulence, an eight-leg day and you can appreciate how tough a job it was. Our Mohawk/Allegheny flight attendants were indeed a class act.

To give you some idea, there is one incident that makes the point. One hot summer night I had a full ship from Philadelphia to Jacksonville, Florida. Climbing through twenty thousand feet, we experienced a shudder, the autopilot disconnected and one bank of engine instruments went to zero with associated warning lights. It was like the hand of God had grabbed hold of the engine. I thought it had fallen off the aircraft. We subsequently learned that a main bearing had seized and the resulting torque could well have ripped the engine off, but it didn't.

I immediately started a descent. Given our heavy weight so soon after takeoff, we could never have maintained that altitude on one engine. We declared an emergency and were given radar vectors back to Philadelphia. I called up Diana, the senior flight attendant, explained what happened, and made a public announcement. I expected no problem on landing but prudence demanded that the passengers be briefed on evacuation procedures and be aware that the airport emergency equipment would follow us down the runway after landing.

Later I learned that Diana and her cohorts not only prepared the cabin, but also served a complimentary cocktail to any passenger that wanted one! She figured if there was a chance of dying we owed them a drink. What a gal.

The landing worked out fine, a grease job, but a heavy DC-9 on a hot summer night is one hell of a big single-engine airplane. I would not have attempted a go-around from low altitude and in the pre-landing briefing I told the first officer and the tower that once we were on low approach we were committed to land. It was a serious decision based on our weight, the temperature and the unknown aerodynamics of the ship. The engine may have shattered its cowling, offering considerably more drag. I had no way of knowing.

The emergency equipment was perfectly positioned and out in force. It is quite a sight and altogether reassuring to know that they are there for you. In a survivable aircraft accident, meaning one in which impact forces are not fatal, fire and smoke are the killers and every second counts. For that reason, there is a special bond between airport firefighters and pilots. They have certainly always had my highest respect and thanks.

Flight dispatch and the Philly station did a great job in finding another ship to press into service and in a short time we boarded it and were on our way. Every passenger chose to continue. Pretty cool. And of course it was free drinks to Jacksonville.

****

The DC-9 was a pre-computer magic airplane. We had Collins FD-109 flight directors, which were pretty sophisticated for their day, and an enunciator overhead panel warning system that was a great improvement. It condensed information that other aircraft like the One Eleven had spread all over the cockpit. Aside from that, it was round gages and a far cry from today's all-glass instrumentation.

The autopilot (A/P) was basic chocolate and vanilla, nothing fancy. It could do a pretty good Instrument Landing System (ILS) coupled approach, but there was no auto land capability. They did install a radio altimeter, and with the FD-109 we were able to operate down to Cat II landing minima. The A/P could track a Visual Omni Range (VOR) radial, but did it poorly and most of us simply flew in a heading mode. Nor could we program climbs and descents and usually used a manually set rate of climb/descent and then altitude hold. By today's standards, it was pretty primitive stuff, but it did the job.

We didn't have area navigational ability or flight management systems, so the pilot was forced to be mentally more spatially oriented. It was great training. The problem the senior pilots had in transitioning to the computer magic airplanes was the overabundance of information; they literally got overloaded and wanted to turn the "stuff" off. The young guys with computer backgrounds had the opposite problem; if you turned the magic off, they got disoriented.

You developed ongoing simple mathematical calculations. Using the Distance Measuring Equipment (DME) and a sweep second hand you could easily calculate your ground speed: One mile in 10 seconds equals 6 miles in 60 seconds, equals 360 miles an hour (360 knots). One mile in six seconds equals 10 miles in 60 seconds, equals 600 miles an hour (600 knots). At 360 knots, it will take you six minutes to travel 36 miles. If Air Traffic Control issued a crossing restriction to be at an altitude 5,000 feet lower 36 miles ahead, you would have to be at that altitude within six minutes. A rate of descent of 1,000 feet per minute would get you there with a minute to spare. In the magic airplanes, you put the restriction in the computer and George does the rest. Truth is, I always did the quick mental calculations anyway as a back up. Survival 101: Never depend upon any single thing.

The flight directors grew out of work in the 1960s to reduce landing weather minima. Evaluating the Collins FD-108 was one of my jobs on the ALPA All Weather Flying Committee. At the time we also looked at flight directors being developed by Sperry and Bendix. All represented a great achievement in avionics. Simply put, the FD displays to the pilot pitch and bank guidance for programmed maneuvers, using moving icons overlaid on the Artificial Horizon (AH). The raw data selected is fed through a computer system to drive the icons.

Prior to flight directors, a pilot's instrument scan on an ILS approach had to range from the AH, a gyro stabilized compass for heading information, vertical speed indicator and ILS cross pointer. The pilot then provided his own pitch and bank guidance. The FD put the information needed on the one instrument and provided computed guidance. It was quite a breakthrough and it was further developed through the Electronic Flight Instrument Systems (EFIS)/ Cato-ray Tube (CAT) technology incorporated in the B-767 and later aircraft.

The DC-9 had the FD-109. The One Eleven and the FH-227 had an earlier version, the FD-108, which was a slightly smaller instrument but worked the same way. Both appeared somewhat three-dimensional, with a fixed orange delta representing the airplane. A calibrated backdrop rotated on both axes to represent pitch and roll. It was blue in the (FD-108) and turquoise in the (FD-109) to represent the sky (up). Black represented the ground (down). Inverted V bars provided the steer guidance; you flew the delta into the V bars. Other type FDs used a separate vertical and horizontal bar and a fixed bar for the aircraft. I felt that the fixed bar, although not as pretty, gave a more precise presentation.

****

I flew the DC-9-31 and -50 (while we had them) until transitioning to the B-727-200 in 1988. By that time I had been with the airline twenty-nine years. After that, I piloted the 727 for three years, flying coast to coast and to Puerto Rico and Bermuda. Then I was in the B-767 for the last six years of my career, flying overseas, mostly to London and Frankfurt. Consequently, three quarters of my career, or about twenty-six thousand hours, was as a local service/regional pilot. That's a lot of takeoffs and landings—easily over twenty thousand, much of it in the Northeast, in some of the most diverse and unfriendly flying weather in the world.

In all modesty, when it came to flying skills, those of us who came up from the early prop-driven aircraft to fly the jets in local/regional service were the top guns in the industry. It was like being a surgeon in a MASH unit; you got a lot of practice.

There was a tremendous amount of turmoil and growth between 1975 and 1988, the thirteen years I flew the Nine. Ed Colodny tiptoed through the minefields that could have destroyed Allegheny and grew the company after deregulation in 1978. With many thanks to Ed Colodny, I never lost a day's pay.

Airlines had become prey for corporate raiders such as Frank Lorenzo and Carl Icahn. As airlines were scooped up with hostile leveraged buyouts, once solid companies such as Eastern, Pan American, Western, Braniff and National ceased to exist.

Icahn beat out Lorenzo in a hostile takeover of Trans World Airlines in 1985. He took the company private in 1988, ran up over half a billion dollars of debt in the process, raped labor and sold off routes. Failing, the airline filed bankruptcy in 1992, struggled along until 2001, when finally American Airlines bought the remains of its assets.

Lorenzo could be the poster boy of rape and blunder airline takeovers. As head of Texas International Airlines, he systematically began acquiring airlines weakened by deregulation, including Continental, New York Air, Frontier Airlines and Eastern Airlines.

Airlines were not the only targets for hostile leveraged buyouts, but they were among the easiest targets. The game went something like this: Have sufficient access to investment capital to purchase a significant position in a corporation, then, by using the company's own assets, bid up the price to acquire control. This was done by arbitrage brokers who fed on successful companies with assets that were easily split off and sold. Needless to say, labor was always raped in the process. Companies eventually learned to protect themselves, but tens of thousands of people lost everything in the process.

Corporate raiders and leveraged buyouts eventually gave way to management cooking the books, drawing huge salaries and bonuses while defrauding stockholders, robbing retirement funds and, as always, screwing labor.

God bless him, Ed Colodny was far from a weak CEO and he managed to hold off the sharks. Unfortunately, after Colodny left the airline in 1991, his successor Seth Schofield would lose the company to a wolf, Stephen Wolf, who took over as CEO of USAir in 1996.

Ed Colodny had a different management style than Les Barnes, but proved to be a good man to work for and, like Les, he earned the respect of labor.

Shortly after Colodny took the reins, I had a run-in with a lead agent and a flight dispatcher at Washington National over a flight to Islip, Long Island. The weather at Islip was good and the dispatcher released the flight with minimal fuel and no alternate. In computing the fuel, the first officer figured we needed several hundred pounds more to be legal and prudent. I agreed and told the agent to advise dispatch that I needed an amended release to reflect the higher fuel load. After going out to the aircraft, the agent radioed that the dispatcher wouldn't amend the release. If I wanted the additional fuel, I could have the fueler put it on, but the dispatcher wouldn't change the release. My response was to advise the dispatcher that if an amended release wasn't forthcoming, I was going to take my crew and leave the airport.

Needless to say, an amended release came right over. Although I never spoke of the incident to another soul with the company, it was truly a test for the new boss. The fact that I never heard more proved he passed the test. He didn't want wimpy captains or foolish fights over turf by a dispatcher.

Much later, in March of 1979, I had another dispatcher call Colodny at home with a request to ask top level FAA in Washington to approve a special jump seat rider. The Three Mile Island nuclear mishap had occurred the day before and Arizona Governor Bruce Babbitt, who had been assigned to the presidential commission to investigate the accident, was aboard my flight to Harrisburg, Pennsylvania. The power plant is in the traffic pattern to the airport and I thought the governor would like to have a front row seat to see it. Ed got the approval and the governor was delighted to look right down the smoke stack from the cockpit. Of course my wristwatch has glowed in the dark ever since!

When asked if I ever had any harrowing experiences, my knee-jerk response is to say no, that it was my job to keep life boring. I always thought of being a captain as risk management; flying was just the fun part. But there were some other memorable experiences that I will share with you.

Shortly after going on the Nine, during a flight to Buffalo, New York, we failed to get a safe green main landing gear light. We abandoned the approach and entered a holding pattern to troubleshoot the system. We replaced the lamps in the instrument, but no dice. There is a way to check the main landing gear visually by lifting the passenger aisle carpet over the wing and viewing the gear locks through a periscope with mirrors. Trouble was, the mirrors were so dirty you couldn't see a thing.

First thing you know there's a radio relayed call from Harvey Thompson, my boss, whom I'd met only once before concerning the security issue at Bradley Field. It was a nice gesture; he was concerned and wanted to know how it was going. I told him what we'd done and that my next step was a control tower flyby so the gear could be checked visually to see if it was extended. There would be no way to know if it was locked. I told Harvey I would call him after landing.

The tower visually confirmed that the gear was extended as we flew by at about fifty feet. That was fun. Normally they'd lock you up for doing that. We swung back around and, with the fire department standing by, we landed. The landing gear was indeed down and locked. I had maintenance pin the gear for additional safety and taxied to the gate. I called Harvey first thing and learned that he had seen the episode on national TV.

The next day there was a campaign to make sure all periscope mirrors were in proper focus, clean and the gear locks freshly painted with a black stripe. Harvey didn't want more publicity.

A few days after my divorce was final in April 1985, I was on TV again with the DC-9. Linda Vatalie, a dear friend, was the lead flight attendant and in cahoots with the other two attendants had planned a special treat. On the way to Bradley Field they came to the cockpit and did a special and modest fashion show of Fredric's of Hollywood erotic ware. Being respectful of art, the first officer hung the items around the cockpit.

Let me tell you, after I saw that a TV crew was meeting the flight, we hardly more than crawled to the gate so the FO would have time to take our art down. After the passengers were off, Frank Petee came on board with the TV crew and a flock of "Fearful Flyers" to do a dry run. If they had seen the cockpit a few minutes before, they would have run all right!

Frank was retired, one of the airline's first pilots and great guy. He ran the airline's fearful flyers program, which was a highly successful progression of hands-on classes to combat fear. It became a model for the industry. When his class had gone, I showed him our art. He laughed his ass off.

Allegheny changed its name to USAir in 1979 to reflect its expanding network to the west. In 1987, Allegheny bought Pacific Southwest (PSA) and in 1988 Piedmont Airlines. With Piedmont came routes to Europe and the wide-body Boeing 767-200. PSA had an extensive presence in California, with hourly flights between Los Angeles and San Francisco. Both PSA and Piedmont had the Boeing 727-200 that I jumped on shortly after the 1987-88 acquisitions. I was restricted from the Piedmont 76 until 1991 because of the pilots' seniority list merger agreement, although I was very senior in years of service on the combined list by that time.

USAir, PSA and Piedmont had all grown quickly in a race to reach a critical survivable mass. Had we not combined, there is no doubt that one or all would have been a trophy for one of the corporate raiders.

In 1986, a radical change in the federal tax law also changed the character of investment capital for the airline industry, and many other industries. Prior to the change, a person or a corporation could count all income against all loses to determine tax liability. After the change, loses could only be counted against the investment capital for that particular activity. This was a major factor in the sale of Piedmont because it was used as a tax shelter for the Norfolk & Southern Railroad.

Norfolk & Southern had financed a fleet of aircraft for Piedmont; including B-767s, which they were able to depreciate against railroad income. The railroad had the money and considerable political clout to win European routes for Piedmont and the big aircraft. An interesting aside is that Piedmont found it necessary to hire pilots with big aircraft experience to satisfy their insurers, who were concerned about lack of experience. A lot of them came from Braniff, which had gone bankrupt and out of business.

USAir and PSA also hired pilots from the failed carriers, which made rapid growth safer and less of a training challenge. Unfortunately, some of them also brought a great deal of bitterness in having to start over again at the bottom of the seniority list. Sadly, the days of favorable pilot-management labor relations at Allegheny/ USAir were numbered.

Three Engines—At Last!

I loved flying the Boeing 727-200. It was big, beautiful and at last I had more than two engines. Better than the computer magic airplanes, it was voice activated: We had a flight engineer. The systems were somewhat primitive but three pilots made a far better flight deck crew.

Boeing's initial design studies of a medium range tri-jet began in 1956 and serious development of the Boeing 727-100 began in 1959. The program was launched on the basis of a combined order from Eastern and United for eighty aircraft in 1960. The prototype flew in February 1963. It was certified in December and entered service with Eastern in February 1964.

The 727-100 is powered by three 14,000 pounds of thrust Pratt & Whitney (P&W) JT8D-7 turbofans, the same engine as the DC-9-10. Maximum takeoff weight is 160,000 pounds with a seating capacity of 131 passengers. It has a wingspan of 108 feet and is 133 feet 2 inches long. The cockpit and fuselage cross section of 12 feet 4 inches is physically identical to the 707, except that the lower section is smaller to carry less luggage for shorter flights. It has a very interesting wing that incorporates triple slotted Kruger flaps and multi-sectioned leading edge slates; the wing literally comes apart as it grows. There were 582 727-100s built.

Within a year Boeing was working on a stretched version, the 727-200. They would incorporate 10-foot plugs forward and aft of the wing, stretching the length to 153 feet 2 inches, and bringing the seating up to 189. The other physical dimensions remained the same and the gross takeoff weight was increased to 209,500 pounds. Several more powerful engines would muscle the –200. The P&W JT8D-9, with 14,500 pounds of thrust, the same engine that powers the DC-9-30. (We had a few of these and they were dogs.) The P&W JT8D-15 (15,500 pounds) was on most of the –200s we had and was also on the DC-9-50. The JT8D-17 (16,000 pounds) was on a hand full of (Advanced) late production models that we operated. They also had some additional fuel capacity for longer range.

The first test flight of a 727-200 was in July 1967, with certification that following November. It entered service with Northeast Airlines in December 1967; Delta Airlines subsequently bought Northeast. Production ceased on the Advanced version in 1984, after a run of about 1,249 727-200s.

US Air Boeing 727-200 executing a missed approach at
Los Angeles International Airport, CA.

Photo by Darrel W. Duarte

A number of 727-100s were upgraded with Rolls Royce Tay engines and used as freighters by United Parcel Service (UPS).

Some 100s are used as large corporate aircraft. The 727-200 was extremely popular and is still in use in the United States and around the world.

****

In the spring of 1988, I entered training on the 72 (as we called the 727-200) at the USAir training center in Pittsburgh. The company had purchased a local elementary school and turned it into a ground school for pilots. They ran some flight attendant training there as well. It was located in a nice residential area in hilly terrain to the west of the airport. The company ran the "Blue Bird," a school bus, on a schedule to pick up and return students from the local hotels we used, the airport terminal, the ground school and the simulator building, which is on the other side of the airport. The ride in the Blue Bird could be memorable. Once the brakes failed while we were barreling downhill; only a skilled driver saved the day by going through the bushes uphill onto somebody's lawn!

USAir grew to over six thousand pilots after the PSA and Piedmont purchases. The route structure sort of looked like a bow tie: heavy on the East and West coasts, skinny in the center of the country, with a few overseas fingers to London, Frankfurt, Bermuda and the Caribbean. The fleet of aircraft included the B-767-200, B-727-200 (in 3 engine configurations), B-737-200/300/400, MD-80, DC-9-30 and the BAe 146 (a 4 engine regional jet that held 70).

The demands on the flight training department were tremendous. And they were no less on maintenance, which was responsible for training and providing parts and support for a large diverse fleet of aircraft. These problems were exacerbated by three decidedly different airline cultures and overstaffing due to duplication. Layoffs were inevitable and deeply resented, as management struggled to bring costs under control.

Because it cost the company so much, airline ground school is like being force fed with a fire hose. Modern jet aircraft are complicated pieces of equipment with many subsystems to learn. A properly trained pilot must conceptually understand every one of those systems and interrelate them into the total aircraft operation. Luckily, pilots don't need to know how to maintain those systems.

Indeed, most mechanics would agree that a screwdriver in a pilot's flight kit is a dangerous weapon.

Most aircraft transition ground schools now run only about ten days, ending with a written test followed by an oral examine given by an FAA designated flight examiner. The training is intense, particularly if you haven't flown the aircraft before as a junior pilot or flight engineer.

I was the only transitioning captain in a class of about eight. We were fortunate to have a few of the school's best ground school instructors; one was a retired TWA captain who had had quite a lot of time in the aircraft. Throughout my career, my modus operandi in training was never to let something go by that I didn't understand. My hand would shoot up and I would ask for clarification. It always paid off. Usually others needed more information as well. They were just afraid someone would think they were stupid if they asked for it.

I aced the written test, did well with the oral, then went on to simulator training. My last aircraft transition had been to the DC-9 thirteen years before. Of course in between I'd taken a check ride in the DC-9 simulator every six months, which amounted to twenty-six check rides. During that time, the airline had built a modern simulator building northwest of the airport. The computer hearts of simulators like dry air at a constant cool temperature. Consequently, the simulator building was built like a bunker, with just the roof above ground. It had bays for about eight pieces of equipment. These are large, tall rooms with the simulator cockpits that are identical to the real aircraft standing on hydraulically powered gimbaled legs and looking like huge spiders. You enter the cockpit through a locking door adjacent to the briefing rooms. The cockpit is over a ramp. Once the system is activated, the door is locked and the ramp withdrawn so that the cockpit cab sitting atop the gimbals is totally free of the building. All view outside the windows is either visually simulated or dark.

By that time, the visual systems had progressed far enough to allow the total training experience, including the certification rating check ride, to be done in the simulator. Initial operating experience would be on scheduled flights with a line instructor/check pilot. It is safe and it works, but it is a unique experience nonetheless.

I trained with a crew transitioning to the other seats, which was great. The first officer and I shared the flight instructor, while the engineer had another instructor, so there were five of us in the simulator as we worked. The engineers' aircraft systems training is more extensive than the pilots'. The 72 does not have the automation of the jets that were designed later for two pilots. There are generators that have to be paralleled, a pressurization system that requires hands-on, a fuel dump system that can only be operated from the engineer's position, and other things similar to the 707.

Sonny Bellman was one of our instructors and he was a piece of work. He and his wife Danny, who was a flight attendant, had more than a few bucks and loved the finer things of life. They had a beautiful home where I was privileged to be a dinner guest, and also an extensive art collection. Sonny was extremely articulate and an excellent instructor. Cockpit communication is vital with a three-man crew and he was indeed a communicator.

There is absolutely no question in my mind that a three-man (or woman) crew is superior on large aircraft. It's a more professional flight deck and better able to cope with managing the flight. Without significant discipline, two pilots can get too chummy; somehow that doesn't happen with three. On the 76, I had an International Relief Officer (IRO), so from 1988 until I retired in 1997 I had a crew of three; although the IRO was not required to be on the flight deck at any time and was simply used by custom when a pilot was resting. Unfortunately, there is no aircraft now being built or planned that requires more than a two pilot crew.

The flight engineer's seat was also a refuge for pilots forced from a flying position by the FAA Age 60 Rule. We had a lot of them and they were a terrific asset. American Airlines blocked them out and it has been in litigation for many years; I testified on behalf of the litigating pilots years ago. As time went on, only a few aircraft in the country's airline fleet required a flight engineer: the B-727, DC-10 and the L-1011.

One of the interesting simulator training maneuvers was a single engine (two engines out) approach to a landing or go-around. The aircraft could maintain altitude and even climb slowly on one engine in a clean configuration; meaning slats, flaps and landing gear retracted.

Fuel would be dumped to reduce weight. It can be pumped at a fast rate through outlet pipes on each wing tip down to standpipes in the fuel tanks, which safeguard sufficient fuel to go around the traffic pattern.

The approach would require almost maximum power on the single engine to maintain a glide path with the gear down and an approach flap setting. To go around, that engine would be firewalled, the gear and flaps retracted, and the aircraft allowed to accelerate down the glide path until sufficient speed was reached to level off and then eke out a climb. It took several hundred feet to do that.

The 72's performance with a single engine failure at V1 is similar to other aircraft, but normal all-engine takeoffs provide less obstacle clearance than the two-engine aircraft does, because a single-engine failure only reduces available power by a third instead half. This was evident during our normal maximum weight takeoffs from San Francisco, when we cleared the dike to San Francisco Bay by about 75 feet. Most captains, including me, would instruct the flight engineer to have his hand on the fuel dump switches. If we lost an engine, he was to start dumping immediately.

I'd had engines fail in every two-engine aircraft I ever flew with the airline. Wouldn't you know that now that I three engines on the 72, I never lost a one.

Myron Bennett gave me my rating ride. I screwed up timing the rate of descent on a nonprecision approach and was too high to land safely, but I was smart enough to execute a highly professional go-around and do it again. I got my ticket. As a check airman, I looked for the same thing in a pilot: The ability to always have options and not be afraid of changing your mind.

I did most of my initial operating experience with Ron Sessa. Prior to that, I had ridden in the jump seat of a 72 once or twice, but had never sat in the pilot's seat. My initial feeling was, "holy shit, this thing is big!" With an aircraft 153 feet 2 inches long, the cockpit is half a football field in front of the tail. On the ground, the wing tip could easily clear an object in a tight turn, but the tail would hit it.

Taxiing too fast in a turn could launch a flight attendant standing in the tail like a stone from a slingshot. They didn't like that.

Ron was patient and a good instructor. One of the things we didn't have in the simulator was the Omega navigational system that was on the aircraft. Omega used a grid of eight or so extremely low frequency, powerful radio stations putting out signals that could be received around the world. If your equipment received two signals or more, three was most desirable, it would triangulate your position on the Earth in latitude and longitude. With help of computers, it could then be used as an area navigational system to go from one point to another. You had to position it to start with and it needed to be updated in flight for improved accuracy.

On our East Coast/West Coast flights, Omega permitted direct routings that saved time and fuel. The Inertia Reference Systems on the later equipment would do the same thing, only a lot better.

You had to be able to enter the data quickly and precisely, which proved a little challenging when flying a ship that was new to you. It took me a couple of flights to feel confident in its use. Otherwise, I loved flying the airplane. The cockpit was a little noisier than the DC-9, and the area around you could get quite cold when at high altitude for a length of time. But it is a pilot's airplane. Landings were kind of fun. With the main wheels so far back, you could time an attitude change on flare by lowering the nose and touch down with the wheels coming up for a grease job. If you timed it wrong, it wasn't so delicate. On the flights back and forth to the West Coast, we had to be careful with the mountain wave effect caused by the continental divide. The westerly winds are lifted up to crest the rocky mountains then cascade down the east side, causing a down draft that extends up to a high altitude. At heavy weights, which was our usual condition, the margin between high and low speed buffet could be small and the power available insufficient to maintain altitude if you reached too far.

Most of us were pretty careful not to cut the buffet margin too close, although the airline did have a few high altitude upsets. Some years before, Hoot Gibson of TWA became infamous with a high altitude upset that damn near tore the aircraft apart. Being an inventive sort of guy, he learned that by pulling a particular circuit breaker he could disassociate the first position of flaps from extending the leading edge slats. A little bit of flap at high altitude increased the low speed stall margin. One unfortunate day, Hoot had the aircraft so configured and left the cockpit to go to the john. The flight engineer, unaware of Hoot's trick, reset the breaker. The leading edge slats deployed and the aircraft fell out of the sky! Thus was born the infamous Hoot Gibson maneuver—definitely not a good thing.

The 72s have two separate hydraulic systems, an "A" system that carries the major loads and a "B" system that offers redundancy to some important systems. It also has two separate rudders, a larger A and a smaller B; either can control the aircraft, with some limitations. Unfortunately, the B-737 didn't have that duplicity. If it had, two tragic accidents might have been avoided.

We did have an A system total failure approaching Boston one day. The landing gear had to be manually lowered using a crank in the floor of the cockpit. That was the flight engineer's work. It takes a gazillion turns to lower the gear. There were other limitations as well, all of which required emergency equipment to stand by. The crew really worked well together, flight deck and cabin, and everything turned out fine.

On October 16, 1989 my crew and I were on an overnight in Los Angeles. We were scheduled to fly to San Francisco and on to Pittsburgh the next morning. During the early morning hours, an extremely destructive earthquake rocked the San Francisco area. Tremors were felt pretty far south, but we didn't experience any in our high-rise hotel, thank God. Our flight was canceled that morning, but we were among the first flights to land in San Francisco the morning after. It was pretty eerie; the airport terminal had sustained a fair amount of damage.

Flying the 72 was good duty and a great transition to the much larger, wide-bodied Boeing 767s that I would fly next. We had some nice overnights, too. One I liked was in San Diego. My wife Sue joined me on one of those, which was great. We got up early and went to the San Diego zoo, one of the world's treasures. Now I use the pith helmet I bought there for yard work around the house. It's cool.

Flying the 72 was also a good entry into over-water operations. I flew quite a few trips to Bermuda, Nassau and Puerto Rico. Having read about the "Bermuda Triangle," I was particularly vigilant, knowing that the sharks in those warmer waters would find a somewhat chubby Italian a delicacy.

Dave Linzinmeir, the Pittsburgh 727 chief pilot, invited me to be one of his line instructor/check pilots. It involved special training and FAA approval, part of which was flying from the right seat when training a captain. It was a way to contribute something I enjoyed doing back to the airline and its pilots.

I was assigned to give initial operating experience to my old buddy Ron Neibauer when he bid over to the 72. Ron is a terrific pilot and we had a nice few days together. He was doing a fine job with the aircraft and I decided to steal a leg from the right seat. This is a little like driving a car with the steering wheel on the right on the left side of the road; it just doesn't feel natural. (As a first officer you don't know any better, so it's all right.) The landing was on runway 33L at Baltimore Washington International (BWI). It was a beautiful day, offering no excuse for dropping the airplane the last few feet to earth. Needless to say, the flight attendants made a big deal of adjusting their bras.

****

There were some notable accidents between 1987 and 1991:

On August 16, 1987, a Northwest MD-82 crashed on takeoff from runway 3C at Detroit Metro Airport, killing 156. It was found that the crew had failed to set the flaps and slats properly. The aircraft stalled, clipped a building and wound up across a road on the northeastern periphery of the airport. Amazingly, an infant child survived.

Shortly after USAir bought Pacific Southwest Airlines (PSA), on December 7, 1987, David Burke, a recently fired USAir employee from Rochester, New York used his then invalid credentials to board a PSA Bae-146 flight with a pistol. He shot both pilots. The pilotless aircraft crashed near San Luis Obispo, California, killing the five crewmembers and 37 passengers.

Used differentially, it induces a skid that creates a turn. For pitch they used the natural trim speed, what engineers call "phugoid." By reducing power, the aircraft loses speed and the nose goes down; increasing power gains speed and the nose goes up.

With the help of a deadheading DC-10 captain, who came forward to physically manage the throttles, they got the aircraft on the ground, if not the runway, at the Sioux City Gateway Airport. When they hit, they were doing 215 knots and accelerating with a sink rate of 1,850 feet per minute. A normal landing would have been at about 140 knots and a sink rate of 200-300 feet per minute. One hundred and twelve people died, but 186 survived, an incredible feat. We recreated the scenario in the B-767 simulator and you can achieve a certain amount of control. Such training is good to have in your repertoire of tricks.

Troubled Airlines, Troubled World

In 1991, Ed Colodny surprised everyone by retiring suddenly as president and CEO of USAir. Looking back, it was probably the wisest personal decision of his life because the writing was on the wall: Increased size alone was not enough for an airline to be profitable and survive. Under his stewardship, USAir had grown tremendously and fought off hostile buyouts. Regardless of his efforts at USAir, the industry was still struggling to cope with deregulation and had focused on labor concessions, particularly from their pilots, to compete with each other and with the nonunion start-up cut-rate airlines. In the long term, labor concessions would prove to be only a Band-Aid as the industry slid toward insolvency.

Professionals of all kinds, always sensitive to the regulatory power of the government, had become the brunt of America's turn to the ideological far right. Airline pilots and doctors proved to be prime, easy targets for the faulted economic ideology the far right promulgated as it cut the throat of the middle class.

It is ironic that while Americans are led to believe that the airline industry is "deregulated" and that the United States doesn't have "socialized" medicine, the government in fact controls both industries. The FAA controls airport slots, air traffic and bilateral agreements with foreign airlines. The Justice Department strictly oversees anti-trust regulations, mergers and prevents price collusion between airlines. The nation's largest health insurers are Medicare and Medicaid. Accordingly, the government strictly controls the price of medical care. It also regulates the powerful health insurance industry and Health Maintenance Organizations (HMOs). To say these industries are not regulated is absurd. They are just badly regulated.

Medicare, Medicaid and the powerful insurance companies have forced doctors, historically self-employed, out of private practice. They have been coerced into HMOs and other employment arrangements with hospitals or other medical groups. At those alternative facilities, with no union, and no collective bargaining power, doctors have suffered the consequences of any nonunion employee, prompting many of them to leave the profession.

After deregulation and Ronald Reagan's PATCO (air traffic controllers' union) debacle, airline pilots became easy prey for the anti-labor forces. Fighting for survival, individual pilot groups turned on each other to gain competitive advantage, rather than rallying around a common cause to fight a system that had become intrinsically anti-labor. ALPA, built around a regulated industry, has proved structurally unable to act with solidarity in a deregulated environment.

The large pilot group at United Airlines chose a different path. The pilots sought to leverage their pension funds with wage concessions to gain control of the airline through an Employee Stock Option Plan (ESOP). A 1989 takeover bid by billionaire Marvin Davis led to a management and union buyout plan that failed. They would succeed in 1994, under CEO Stephen Wolf. Prior to going to United, Wolf had engineered the demise of Republic Airlines and Flying Tigers. Republic was sold to Northwest Airlines, Flying Tigers to FedEx. His modus operandi was to groom an airline for sale by ramming through large labor concessions and then selling the carrier.

After the pilots gained control of United, they dumped Wolf, but he would emerge again, replacing Schofield at USAir in 1996. His mission was always the same: to rape labor and merge or sell the airline. Both United and US Airways slid into Chapter 11 bankruptcy in 2003. Wolf and his sidekick Rakesh Gangwal, who came with him from United to be president of USAir, drew $15 million apiece as a separation bonus. The pilots' pension plan, on the other hand, was terminated. Disgracefully, the ALPA pilots at US Airways agreed to management's plan, effectively screwing retired pilots and their families. Behind it all, the Bush administration pulled the strings by dangling a guarantied loan that required the company to terminate its pension plan or lose the loan. Ironically, the financial group investing in the plan was the Alabama pension fund. How's that for union integrity!

Seth Schofield became CEO of USAir in 1991, after Ed Colodny left. Seth had come up though the operational ranks, starting with Allegheny as a station agent. He was personable and well liked by the pilots. Colodny had advanced Seth steadily up the corporate ladder to be his executive vice president, so when the board elevated him to president it was no surprise; the directors were looking for labor concessions and they figured he was the guy to get them. Unfortunately, Seth's comradeship with the USAir pilots didn't carry forward to either the Piedmont or PSA groups. Despite Colodny and Schofield's broad use of Piedmont and PSA managers, those pilot groups fought them at every turn. It proved to be a difficult marriage of radically different cultures.

USAir had achieved mass but had too many equipment types, too many employees and too many unprofitable routes. The company was bleeding cash and had to change to survive. Schofield tried everything: larger hubs at Pittsburgh, Philadelphia and Charlotte, bigger aircraft, smaller aircraft, grounded aircraft, abandoned routes, furloughed pilots, and he entered into a code sharing agreement with British Airways (1993-1996). Although he did get some labor concessions, they were not enough for the board of directors; he was replaced by Wolf (the labor predator) in 1996.

As Schofield duked it out with the unions, there were some other major setbacks for the airline. The first Gulf War in 1991 whacked international air travel. That would happen again in spades when the United States invaded Iraq in 2003. USAir also suffered several accidents that showered the airline with negative publicity. In 1991, a collision in Los Angeles killed 32. A year later an improperly deiced F-28 at La Guardia crashed on takeoff, killing 27. In 1994, a DC-9 at Charlotte crashed while attempting a go-around, killing 37. And then there was the 1994 tragedy, when that 737 crashed on approach to Pittsburgh, killing everyone on board (134).

The proliferation of computers and the Internet during the decade of the 1990s also had a profound effect on air travel. Business could be conducted online and by e-mail cheaply and quickly, often eliminating the need to travel. Business people also found themselves in cramped seating and crowded surroundings as airlines jammed more seats on the aircraft and cut back on service. By not meeting the limited criteria for cheap fares, business travelers also pay top dollar, the cost hardly set off by frequent flyer miles given the traveling employee. Overall, the need for travel fell more and more to the higher echelons of management, who became less tolerant of airline service. This helped create a wave of corporate jet cooperatives, which allowed a company access to an aircraft at a fraction of the cost of 100 percent ownership.

The Internet and computer arts also resulted in marketing schemes that sold seats as a commodity unto itself, to a large extent void of any airline brand name. Today's airline passenger could easily find that no two fellow passengers have paid the same fare. The goal is to put butts in seats, but if in the end the flight doesn't make money, it is not a sound business plan.

****

When George Bush the elder took office as president in 1989, the economy wasn't in great shakes, either. President Ronald Reagan (1981-89) had cut taxes for the rich and dramatically increased defense spending, running up the national debt from $1 trillion to $3.5 trillion in eight years. Reaganomics, as his economic plan came to be known, purported that tax cuts given to the rich would "trickle down" and stimulate the economy. That theory has also been dubbed supply side economics. President John Kennedy had proposed the same thing, except with Reagan it was a ruse. The real goal was to bankrupt the Soviet Union by outspending it militarily. He certainly did that and passed the debt on to future generations. President George W. Bush is doing the same thing in 2003—tax cuts for the rich and deficit spending to fund a war on Iraq. Exactly what we will win or lose is still at question. In the summer of 2003, we were looking at a budget deficit of $455 billion, the largest in history.

Reagan left us another legacy as well—the Savings & Loan debacle. The S&Ls, also called thrifts, originated in Great Britain and came to the United States in the 1930s. S&Ls collected deposits, paid interest and loaned the money out in twenty to thirty year mortgages to finance homes. Because the interest paid was lower than the interest charged, the S&Ls made money. Commercial banks, on the other hand, were restricted by the Federal Reserve Board to pay 3 percent or less on deposits The S&Ls were not restricted and paid 11/2 to 2 percent more to attract funds and charged 21/2 to 3 percent more on mortgages, which generated a comfortable profit.

In the 1970s, some say due to inflation caused partly by the Arab oil embargo and cartel pricing, interest rates zoomed and put a squeeze on the S&Ls holding low interest mortgages. In 1980, Congress phased out interest rate ceilings and allowed the thrifts to diversify into areas theretofore prohibited. Congress also increased the federal deposit insurance to $100,000. Those changes didn't work and, under Reagan, legislators permitted even more flexibility and weakened federal regulatory controls as well. While S&Ls in Texas and California tripled in size between 1982-1985, the Reagan administration reduced the Bank Board's regulatory and supervisory staff. A starting examiner was paid only $14,000 a year and the average experience on the job was two years. The door to the nation's treasury was wide open and it led to wheeling and dealing of massive proportions, with figures such as Charles Keating going to jail and political figures coming under scrutiny for campaign contributions. There were the famous "Keating Five" senators, who collectively received $1.3 million from Keating.

By the time Reagan left and Bush entered office in 1989, Bush faced a disaster as hundreds of S&Ls became insolvent. One of his first acts was to propose a $126 billion bailout to cover insured depositors. It would ultimately cost the American taxpayers over $90 billion after seized assets were liquidated. But there were other costs that cannot be calculated: lost jobs and careers, the unproductive loss of capital and the diversion of savings into excessive overbuilding of office space, inflated prices paid for real estate, and loans on wastelands. America had been successfully swindled.

While some historians credit Ronald Reagan's military build-up and tough stand on the "Evil Empire," as he termed the Soviet Union, with the end of the Cold War, I think that was only a factor. I give a lot of credit to Mikhail Gorbachev, leader of the USSR from 1985-1991. He earned the Nobel Peace Prize in 1990 for his work. He encouraged an independent press with his policy of "glasnost," or openness, for the first time since the Russian Revolution. He cultivated unprecedented close relationships with both Presidents Reagan and Bush, and supported the United States during the Gulf War, just prior to his overthrow from power in 1991. Gorbachev's unwillingness to use force in support of East Germany's Erich Honecker led to Honecker's political demise and to the fall of the Berlin Wall in 1989.

Gorbachev, a believer in democratic socialism, instituted "Perestroika" in 1987, with the goal of restructuring the Soviet system and stripping it of the dehumanizing distortions suffered under the likes of Joseph Stalin and Leonid Brezhnev. He failed and the USSR unraveled instead. Boris Yeltsin took power and the Union of Soviet Socialist Republics ceased to exist as the republics left the federation and became independent; Yeltsin remained as president of Russia and the Russian economy was in for a rough ride.

The coincident end of the Cold War and the limited victory following the rapid end to the Gulf War (the ground war lasted 100 hours) gave the world a tremendous sense of optimism. U.S. allies paid about 80 percent of the cost of the Gulf War, which freed the United States from incurring a large war debt. That was a good thing, because when President Bill Clinton took office in 1993 his biggest challenge was a huge budget deficit and the highest national debt in history.

During the Clinton administration (1993-2001), the United States experienced the largest and longest economic expansion in the history of the country. By 1996, the huge deficit was brought under control and the country was solidly in the black. By the time Clinton left office in 2001, we were enjoying large surpluses. Whom should we credit? Clinton was a fiscal conservative, and some would say not much of a Democrat, but I think he did an excellent job with the economy. Interestingly, from 1995 until he left office, conservative Republicans controlled both houses of Congress. Who can forget Newt Gingrich, the flamboyant archconservative who was Speaker of the House form 1995-1999? Fortunately, the religious far right that controlled Congress spent most of its time attacking Bill Clinton's sex life, which apparently kept it from other mischief. And if you have a perverse sense of humor like I do, the Monica Lewinsky fiasco, although absolutely stupid in the eyes of the world, was nonetheless highly amusing.

Whatever other faults President Bill Clinton may have had, I give him, Treasury Secretary Robert Rubin and Federal Reserve Chairman Alan Greenspan high marks for fiscal policy. They showed that good government could expand the economy without slashing public programs and still balance the budget—something that the ultraconservative far right has yet to demonstrate.

Although the 1990s brought genocide, conflicts and terrorists attacks in much of the world, including the United States, the Clinton administration responded with considerable restraint and diplomacy, using the UN, NATO and other allies. Could we have done better? Sure.

Although it may seem that I have digressed from a story about an airline career, bear with me. I am an amateur historian as well, and the airline industry and I were part of the world around us. The airlines are particularly sensitive to world events and the economy. Clearly, the airlines muddled on through the 1990s, buoyed by the robust economy, when in fact most carriers were in trouble already because of poor government policies originating with deregulation in 1978. Predatory and weak management didn't help much either.

A Machine Seeking Its Element

With thirty-two years of service, I was near the top of the combined USAir seniority list by 1991. The bidding restrictions that gave former Piedmont pilots priority to the Boeing 767s had been satisfied and by early spring I was assigned a training class. Up until that time, Piedmont had used Boeing's ground school and simulators. In the interim, until USAir got its own simulator, we continued to use Boeing, along with TWA's training facilities at Kansas City and Northwest Aerospace Training Corporation (NATCO) outside of Minneapolis. NATCO belonged to Northwest Airlines, which used the facility both to train their pilots and to do contract training.

Contract airline training for pilots and mechanics was becoming a lucrative business. USAir did quite a bit, as did the Pan American Training Institute (PATI) with facilities at JFK. PATI spun off of Pan American World Services in 1987. Flight Safety International, located at La Guardia, did a lot of corporate pilot training. In 1997, Flight Safety, by then a unit of Berkshire Hathaway (Warren Buffet), created a new joint venture company for airline training with the Boeing Company called Flight Safety Boeing Training International.

I would be in the second or third group of pilots going to NATCO under the newly FAA approved USAir program; the only trouble was we had no books or manuals. We used the Boeing manuals and faked it. All of the instructors were former Piedmont guys. Sam

Proctor was mine. There was a little apprehension as we senior USAir originals went into the 76 program. Many of us went to the top of the list rather than the bottom. But most of those involved understood that that was the deal. We had been restricted since the merger four years earlier, but once on the ship we were in seniority. The Piedmont instructors and check pilots were topnotch and I never felt any resentment.

Several weeks prior to starting school at NATCO, I learned that Sam would be my instructor and I called him to ask if he had any study material because the company had none. He had the whole Boeing set of training tapes, about ten 90-minute lectures on VHS. He sent them to me and I had them copied and returned the originals. They were a complete ground school in themselves, covering every system in the aircraft.

By 1991, my mother lived with us most of the time in Littleton, New Hampshire. She suffered from macular degeneration, which had progressed to the point were she had very limited vision. She also had Parkinson's disease and that was not responding well to medication. Mother would sit in a rocking chair and listen for hours while I viewed the Boeing lectures. Ever the encourager, she said she was amazed that I could understand the lectures. After several weeks of it, I think she could have passed the ground school herself!

****

Shortly before Carol filed for a divorce in June 1983, I moved to a chalet on 175 acres with a large pond on the outskirts of Littleton. I had bought the property several years earlier. The local economy was extremely depressed, with double digit inflation that closed businesses, called in mortgages and forced bankruptcies. Unemployment was sky high. When I bought the property, the men who helped out plowing, doing grounds work and supplying firewood approached me for permission to log there. I had done well with rental properties in Marblehead and at the time was looking for other business opportunities. I agreed and established a company called Highlands Wood Products.

It turned out to be a fiasco. Logging is equipment intensive and dangerous. The men needing work had no equipment or the money to buy it. Giant four-wheel articulating machines called skidders drag the logs out of the woods. Even used ones cost many thousands of dollars.

From the landing, articulating hydraulic cranes with claws load the logs on trucks. Buying the loaders and the trucks could bust almost anyone's bank.

Wood products can be broken down into the general categories of: saw logs for lumber; lower quality logs to be processed into pulp for paper products; wood chips used for pulp and electric power generation, and firewood.

There is little or no virgin forest in northern New Hampshire. Almost all wood lots have been harvested for generations. A wood lot is logged in one of two ways; it can be selectively cut or clear-cut. Either way, a logger is committed by contract with the property owner to cut and sell all the wood. My plan was to turn firewood into a profit center, since there are so few saw logs, and hopefully break even on the other products.

Unfortunately, I was truly a babe in the woods and, try as I might, I could never find a manager to make it work. I naively bought equipment such as the skidders and rented them to operators on a lease/purchase agreement against wood produced. I would get a few weeks or a month of production; the loggers would make some money and then vanish. At the time, no manufacturer offered a mill for processing firewood and doing it by hand with chain saws and splitters is extremely labor intensive. I also learned that Workmen's Compensation Insurance for workers in the logging industry would cost half again their wages.

Highlands did cut and sell a lot of wood, even shipping trailer loads of firewood amounting to thousands of cords to distributors in Massachusetts. The only trouble was we lost money on every stick we ever sold. The local bank I did business with also covered itself well, at my expense, by using my personal assets as collateral against equipment loans made at exorbitant interest rates. All this came to a head when Carol filed for divorce. That process froze all my assets so I couldn't simply liquidate the business and take a loss. I was stuck between that proverbial rock and a hard place.

I struggled unsuccessfully with running the business for a year longer, but was finally forced to file Chapter 11 bankruptcy in June 1984. The rental properties in Marblehead and the 175-acre property and chalet in Littleton were lost, but the home in Long Beach was saved and passed on to Carol as part of the divorce settlement. No worker lost a penny and the secured creditors for the most part were paid in full. At the age of 47, I was left penniless, but still with a good job. The business had cost me half a million dollars, as had the total settlement with Carol. I blame no one. I was responsible, but it was an expensive lesson. I tried to do the right thing for the community and failed. Show me someone who's never failed at something and I'll show you someone that hasn't done much. You just can't let it hold you down and I didn't. We still live in Littleton and both Sue and I are deeply engaged in the community.

****

All told, 1983 was quite a year. Sue's parents, who lived outside of Baltimore, and mine had never met until they joined us at the chalet in early fall. Sue's dad was a world famous fisherman and rod maker and our pond was loaded with large and small mouth bass. We had a little rowboat and he and my dad took it out one early evening to fish. Sure enough, the little boat capsized when one of them stood to take a leak and into the water they went. This was dangerous for dad because he'd had surgery for cancer of the larynx ten years earlier and was a neck breather through a stoma (an open tube into the larynx). They were near shore and able to wade in but had gotten terribly cold and wet through. Both went to the hospital and were treated for hypothermia. To say it scared us silly would be an understatement.

The long weekend over, both sets of parents went home and I went back to work flying. After a week or so, Mother said my father was having back pain and guessed possibly he had hit his back when they got dunked, or maybe had gotten too cold. Some days later he was in trouble; he couldn't pass urine and their doctor had admitted him to Maimonides Hospital. I was on a four-day trip and it seemed his care was under control, but I was wrong. I should have gotten relieved and gone to his bedside as soon as possible. Father only had a limited ability to speak from his esophagus because his larynx had been removed and he wasn't getting through to the doctors.

Because he couldn't pee, he was put in the care of an urologist who determined that his prostate gland had a cancerous tumor that was blocking his urine from passing. In the meantime, Father was constantly trying to tell them that his back hurt and he was being ignored. The day before I got down to the hospital they had done radical surgery and removed the gland and his testicles as well; that was the protocol of the day for advanced prostate cancer. It was a bullshit diagnosis.

When I got there and listened to him, he was still complaining about pain in his back, even after major surgery on another part of his body. I went berserk and I certainly had no problem with my voice—the hospital staff heard it loud and clear! Finally somebody looked at his back and took X-rays. He had a spinal lymphoma (cancerous tumor) that was squeezing his nerve trunk. That's why he couldn't urinate; the nerve impulses weren't getting through. He in fact was in the process of being paralyzed from the waist down. He required emergency neurosurgery to remove the tumor.

Even then the medical profession was being turned upside down and Maimonides and other big city hospitals had many foreign nationals practicing. Father's neurosurgeon was from India and to say we weren't on the same wavelength would be an understatement. Father survived the lengthy surgery but it was too late; the delay in treatment had left him paralyzed from the waist down.

After several days, he was transferred to another local hospital for longer term care. Understaffed, with mostly Haitian nurses, the place wasn't terribly clean or well kept. Mother, Sue and I, along my daughter Danielle, visited him on Christmas Day. I had snuck in a small bottle of brandy to celebrate. Father only had a taste, which wasn't like him at all. We talked about the home care he would need, which would require almost full-time help. He had no bladder or bowel control and no sensation in his legs. Mother certainly wasn't strong enough to lift him. But he knew we would do whatever was necessary to get him home. That was the last time I saw my father alive.

Early the next morning we left Brooklyn for Littleton, about an eight-hour drive. We'd picked up Danielle at her mother's house in

Long Beach to spend the Christmas week with us. That afternoon we stopped to eat at a restaurant in Connecticut and I called Mother. Actually, I had a premonition that something was wrong. When Rae Romano, Mother's neighbor and dear friend, answered the phone crying, I knew my premonition was confirmed. Father had died shortly after we left to drive north. He had developed bedsores and a doctor was lancing some boils when my father went into cardiac arrest and died.

The stress of Father's death took its toll on Mother. Within weeks, her vision blurred as blood vessels in the center of the macular in both eyes bled, causing irreversible damage. Thereafter, she had only peripheral vision and her beloved sewing came to an end.

We never sought legal redress for Father's unprofessional and unforgivable medical treatment, but we certainly didn't think it a tragedy when the family doctor who treated him was indicted for Medicare fraud and malpractice. I'll also never be convinced that drastically limiting the right to sue for malpractice is a legitimate way to cut medical costs. What the system needs is sensible limitations that protect doctors from nuisance suits and huge, emotional jury awards.

Mother kept the family home for another seven years or so, while spending more and more time with us in Littleton. Sue and I also made frequent trips to Brooklyn. We hired mother's friend and housekeeper Camille to spend time with her on most days. Camille was much younger than Mother and had come from a town in Italy not far from Mother's. They had a great relationship that allowed Mother to stay in her home for a lot longer than would have been possible otherwise. Sometime around 1992, however, her Parkinson's symptoms require her to be with us and near her medical care full time.

****

With all that behind, back to 1991 and 767 training. NATCO was a huge facility housing simulators for all the different types of aircraft Northwest operated, along with lecture halls and video training equipment. Working in pairs, we viewed training films before going to lectures on the same material; again, it was a little like getting force fed with a fire hose. Boy, I was sure glad I'd gotten to study the Boeing tapes before. That was really a leg up. I was senior in the class and as always not shy about asking questions. I had long since found that there is really no such thing as a dumb question. If something is clarified for you, it usually helps others as well.

The company housed us at a Marriott Residence Hotel not far from the school. We each had a suite with a small kitchen and seating area. They also provided a rental car that was shared by groups of two or three pilots in training. It was a good setup. Not only was it comfortable, but also it enabled evening study after a meal in the room, rather than going out every night to eat. Of course sometimes we'd get together for a meal and do a cookout on the inexpensive barbecue grills we bought. Most of us went home on weekends.

I had developed a bothersome cough that I couldn't seem to shake. The doctor treated me for bronchitis, but I coughed on anyway. I certainly wasn't going to interrupt my training because of it. I learned how serious it was within weeks of completing the training and flying trips to Europe.

The former Piedmont check airman who gave me my several hour oral examine was very thorough, but I was prepared, did well and was signed off. The next step was simulator flight training and I finally got to meet Sam Proctor in person. Sam was slight of build and wiry with a fantastic dry sense of humor. Shortly after he arrived his wife, then a flight attendant with the airline, came to spend a day or two with him. She brought their dog, a little yorkie they called Muttsy or some such. Sam's dry sense of humor, something of legend, includes a story of him sitting in the jump seat giving a line check with Muttsy in a carry case along with him for the ride. The captain really branged the landing; Sam, while saying nothing to the captain, asked Muttsy if he was OK.

My training mate was one of the chief pilots from Charlotte and a friend of Sam's; they lived in a Piedmont pilot enclave outside of town on Lake Norman. It wasn't long into our first training session when I knew I had a problem—they talked so fast I couldn't understand them! Generally, when you think of Southerners, you think of a southern accent and slow speech. Not true. That evening, over a cocktail, I convinced them that they had to talk more slowly for me or this kid from Brooklyn was going to crash and burn. They did and the next day went a lot smoother.

Crew coordination is essential in the 76; it takes two pilots working together to do the job. Each segment of the flight has to be programmed in the Flight Management Computer (FMC), and then each change programmed again; in training the flight profile is changing all the time. An example is an engine failure on takeoff: The FMC would most likely be loaded for a short local flight, say from Boeing Field to an airport 100 miles away. The flying pilot has his hands full flying the airplane, which is always the first priority— screwing with the FMC and flying the aircraft into the ground isn't a winning strategy. The nonflying pilot also has a lot to do, emergency check lists and normal check lists to read, communications to make, call outs and a ton of other things. One of which is to reprogram the FMC—depending on weather—to return to the airport or proceed to a takeoff alternate. After that, the other pilot has to program the navigational radios and program the proper approach in the FMC. Even in clear weather, the Inertia Reference System (IRS) would permit you to build an approach on the FMC without other radio navigational aids.

It can be a busy, busy cockpit, a cockpit that requires two functioning pilots to fly safely. That means the aircraft should have a three pilot crew to safeguard against the possibility of a pilot being incapacitated. The only reason the FAA doesn't require three pilots is cost, pure and simple. As I have said, few people know that the FAA has a double legal mandate: One, as everyone knows, is to promote and regulate safety. The other almost no one knows. Believe it or not, it is to promote air commerce. Safety costs money, so does one mandate collide with the other? The answer is yes, and very frequently.

As one of the founders and an officer of the Professional Pilots Federation (PPF), I took on the FAA, the Clinton administration, most airlines, the Air Line Pilots Association and the Allied Pilots Association over another, but related crew compliment and civil rights issue—the FAA Age 60 Rule. PPF was incorporated just before my training at NATCO; I was a member of the board of directors and elected vice president. The organization still exists; its mission to overturn the Age 60 Rule is still unfulfilled. I resigned from the office just before I retired in 1997. More on PPF and the Age 60 Rule later in the story.

****

The actual simulator flight training program encompassed eight sessions, each lasting four hours, two hours dedicated to each pilot. Because I was training with another captain, we worked two hours, took a break, and then traded seats, with the captain of the moment sitting on the left, of course. The idea is to expose each pilot equally to the whole plethora of maneuvers, failures, fires, instrument approaches and other drills that are part of the FAA certification check ride that follows the training. Each session is like an orchestrated ballet, with one maneuver and drill leading immediately into another. There is simply no time to waste. And you are working all the time, either as the flying pilot or acting first officer.

It is physically and mentally exhausting. The cockpit cab, freed from its ramp tether to the building, rocks and rolls atop giant hydraulic gimbals, creating highly realistic sensations similar to the airplane, sometimes violently. All the instrumentation and systems are not only identical to the airplane but so precisely programmed that simulators are now a prime tool in staging accident investigation scenarios. State of the art visual simulation creates actual airports with runways, taxiways and gates, or even near misses with other aircraft in flight. Turbulence, winds and visibility are manipulated at will. Engine failures, fires, and other system failures are just like the real thing, along with all the bells and whistles.

The instructor works just as hard as the trainees. At an elaborate panel behind the captain's seat, he has to position, orchestrate and run the simulator while at the same time teaching. It's a tough job and Sam Proctor did it extremely well. Somehow or other, at the end of the eight sessions my training partner and I were ready for the FAA check ride. At each airline the FAA designates check airman to do the actual certification. Jimmy Powers, a little guy with a moustache and a reputation as a tough check airman, gave me my ride. It was fair and thorough and the Boeing 757/767 were added to my ticket. The 757 and 767 have sufficient similarity so that the rating covers both, although the 76s are considerably larger. USAir operated quite a few 75s, but I only flew the 76 in international service. The NATCO simulator we trained in was a 76. Later USAir got its own 75 simulator, which I experienced during six-month checks. That's the only time I ever flew the 75. By comparison to the 76, it was kind of a sports car. With the rating in my pocket, there was just one more simulator task, a staged line trip as preparation for the real thing. I had several days off in between and rather than my returning home to New Hampshire, Sue and her youngest brother Bob drove out to spend a couple of days with me. Bob lives in Pikesville, Maryland and picked her up in Littleton for the drive. With fourteen year difference in age, Sue didn't get to know him much as a kid so the times they share now are highly valued. As an only child, I continue to find Sue's siblings a treasured expanded family. I showed them the NATCO facility and, thanks to one of the technicians, gave them a ride in a DC-9 simulator. The 76 was in use. I hadn't flown the nine in several years but it fit like an old shoe. I let Sue and Bob swap off as my co-pilot. They had a great time, nearly jumping out of their skin when the technician staged a near miss!

The early summer weather was pleasant, so we headed north up Interstate 35 to Duluth, then up the west bank of Lake Superior on Route 61, stopping well short of Grand Portage on the Canadian boarder. We passed giant dock facilities where huge Great Lakes ships are loaded with taconite pellets made from taconite iron ore mined at iron ranges west of Lake Superior. Taconite was considered waste rock when high-grade natural iron ore was plentiful. Now that the high-grade ore is no longer plentiful, the process developed to create pellets saved Minnesota's iron ore mining industry. The pellets are transported by railroad cars to giant loading docks at Port of Superior, Two Harbors, Taconite Harbor and Silver Bay, where it is literally dumped into Great Lakes ore ships and transported through locks and canals to the lower Great Lakes, then on to Gary, Indiana, Cleveland, Ohio and other steel-making towns. These days the United States makes so little steel that much of the taconite is probably shipped overseas.

After Sue and Bob left to drive home, Sam Proctor returned from Lake Norman so we could complete the required simulator staged line trip. At this point, with our ratings in hand, the pressure was off and a laugh or two in order. Lord forgive us, the observer we had for the session became an easy target for our warped sense of humor. His name forgotten, although he was a nice guy, he had been selected to be the training commander for the new 76 programs in Pittsburgh. Needless to say, my training partners and I were completely under whelmed with his presence. By that time, we could just about read each other's mind as hands flew around the cockpit. We were a pretty hard act for him to keep track of.

Being the senior pilot, I did the first part of the session, which was a flight to San Francisco. Along the way, Sam threw various systems problems at us that I handled well and he asked if I'd like to try a dead stick (no power) landing. We had trained for multiple engine flameouts at high altitude wherein, during the course of a high dive, the Auxiliary Power Unit (APU) was started to power the electrical and hydraulic systems and one or both of the engines restarted, but we never worked the exercise to a no power landing. An Air Canada 76 had actually run out of fuel and successfully accomplished a dead stick landing at a remote airport in Canada. I had read of the pilot's technique. It was the same that I had used when I dead sticked my J-3 in that potato patch in Rhode Island many years before.

Several thousand feet over San Francisco, Sam failed both engines after creating a clear day with the airport below. The 76 has a wind-driven hydraulic motor that automatically deploys in such a situation to power the flight controls and in short order we were able to start the APU and restore other electrical and hydraulic services. The airplane has a beautiful wing and I knew that if I extended more than an initial flap setting, with no power on the ship, we would develop a high sink rate that would be impossible to recover from. So I flew the approach like a J-3, albeit an enormous J-3.

I deliberately came up to the approach lights several hundred feet high. With no power, I sure as shit wasn't going to risk undershooting. By now our observer was bouncing up and down and telling Sam I was going to overshoot the airport. Sam quietly reassured him. When the runway was made, I put the airplane into a forward sideslip, bled off the altitude, straightened it out and landed smoothly at exactly the right touchdown point, then used a high-speed turnoff to clear the runway. Pretty neat.

For some reason, our new training commander didn't stick around for my partner's flight. By now we'd had about as much fun as we should for one day and his flight was a short one. My training partner would return to Charlotte and retire young, not too long thereafter. Sam also retired early and worked for NATCO instructing on the 75/76. Both feared that the USAir retirement fund wouldn't be there for them—a decade later they'd be proved right. As for me, I'll always fondly recall the time I spent with him and Sam that summer.

****

USAir followed the example of other airlines and divided the international flying to Europe into a separate bid to accommodate working under different Federal Air Regulations and duty time limitations. Transoceanic flying also requires special training that is not part of the normal ground school or simulator training. Piedmont had developed over-water operational procedures that were exceptionally good and had been adopted by other airlines. Almost everything to do with flight planning and FMC management was crosschecked by two pilots to avoid error. As with all computers, garbage in means garbage out and an error in either flight planning or entering information into the flight management computer could put the aircraft miles off course and in someone else's airspace. The training was only a couple of days but excellent. We also had special training in the use of the life rafts and ocean ditching procedures.

The additional training done, I was ready for my first line flight. Mind, I had never before set foot in an actual Boeing 767-200ER. I would be in the left seat with a line check pilot (the job I had on the 727) in the right, and as on all USAir's overseas flights there would be an International Relief Officer (IRO).

My first flight was from Pittsburgh to Frankfurt, Germany with 225 passengers and crew. As I walked up the external stairs on the jetway, I couldn't believe the size of the airplane! I'd never been up close to one and it was immense. The cockpit door from the cabin is hinged on the left and opens in. There is a step up into the cockpit that no one had bothered to tell me about. Of course I managed to trip on it. (On the 757 the step is down.) Nothing inspires confidence as much as the captain falling into the cockpit!

US Airways Boeing 767-200ER after take off from Philadelphia International Aitport.

Photo by Cary Liao

I put my bags down and took a walk around the cabin. Behind the cockpit there is the main passenger door/emergency exit on the left side and a emergency exit/service door opposite, a galley and a lavatory and bulkhead. The front cabin section behind was configured as a business class and pretty plush, two aisles with two seats outside and two in the middle; in the rear cabin, there are three seats in the middle, the section separated by a mid-cabin bulkhead with two lavatories, one on either side. There are two more lavatories in the rear, a larger galley and two more emergency exit/service doors. The ship is 155 feet long and it looked like you could do laps around the two aisles!

Once in the captain's seat I felt more at home, until I looked out. It was like sitting atop an apartment building. The visual presentation in the simulator just didn't give you the same perspective. Fortunately, the check pilot and the IRO helped me stumble through loading a lengthy transoceanic flight into the FMC for the first time, run the check lists and do all the other things required before getting under way.

All that done, the aircraft pushed back from the gate and, engines running, it was time to taxi out to the runway. Now this is a machine 155 feet long with a wing span of 156 feet, 1 inch, none of which you can see from the cockpit. Drawn as a square, it would cover over 24,000 square feet. Consequently, you taxi with extreme care. With the main trucks of wheels 65 feet behind the nose wheel, turns have to be judged accordingly or else you wind up with a main wheel in the dirt. For instance, a maximum effort 180-degree turn, such as reversing direction on a runway could just barely be made in the 150-foot width of most runways. With the nose wheel on centerline, the wing tips hang over the sides of the runway. It is also difficult to judge taxi speed, so you have to constantly refer to instrumentation ground speed, which, fed data by the Inertia Reference System is accurate from zero knots up. Our procedure was to taxi no faster than 20 knots on a straightaway and no more than 10 knots in a turn on a dry surface.

The takeoff would be at the maximum gross weight of 351,000 pounds on runway 10R. The runway is 11,500 feet (over two miles) long. I would have been happier if it were three miles long! We configured the aircraft for optimum takeoff performance for the runway length and weight with leading edge slats and one degree of flaps; the reference speeds for takeoff were V1 160 / VR 164 / V2 168; equated to statute miles per hour from knots, we would lift off at just under 200 MPH. That's mighty fast to be boogying down a thin strip of concrete with 175 tons of metal, fuel and humanity. I would learn that most of my transoceanic flights would be at maximum gross weights. An aborted takeoff at or just before V1 would use every inch of that two-mile runway if attempted. My Charlotte training partner did make a high speed abort at Charlotte. He stopped successfully on the runway, but all eight main tires exploded from the heat.

The B-767-200ER has a useable fuel capacity of 137,000 pounds, or 20,450 U.S. gallons; the fuel density is 6.7 pounds/U.S. gallons. The left or right wing tanks hold 40,700 pounds each and the center tank 55,700 pounds. The average fuel consumption is 10,000 pounds, or about 1,500 gallons per hour, which is extremely efficient. With a full fuel load, the ship has a range of about 6,000 miles, but in the six years I flew that airplane I never once had that much fuel. There would be little weight left over for revenue.

An airplane on takeoff is a machine seeking its element; it comes alive as it picks up speed. The big clumsy pelican on the ground becomes beautiful and graceful in flight. And so it was with the 76, my big apartment house to taxi was terrific to fly. The simulator hadn't done it justice and I loved the airplane from the start.

I had a line check pilot with me for a few more trips, as I grew more comfortable with the ship, transoceanic procedures and European air traffic control. As I said earlier, it was the best duty I ever had with the airline and I enjoyed every minute of it. Except that my cough was getting worse. Bob Peraino, my friend and physician in Littleton, had taken chest X-rays and prescribed different medications, to no avail. After a half a dozen trips across the pond, I was on some asthma medication. But I knew I was in trouble when I almost passed out getting off the airplane in Pittsburgh.

That night back home in Littleton the calf of my left leg hurt a little. The next day it hurt some more so I took a couple of Tylenol, which helped a little. I thought I had banged it or something. By the next day, it hurt like hell and was swollen. Bob was out of town, but fortunately another local surgeon who had treated Mother said to come right in to the hospital. He took one look and admitted me; it was a serious phlebitis (an inflammation of the veins). The cough was caused by blood clots formed by the inflammation going up into my lungs. This was confirmed by a radioisotope scan that showed my lungs laced with small blood clots—a close call because a big clot will put your lights out.

Now the mysterious cough that had plagued me since early spring and during the training at NATCO was explained. That March I had attended a Professional Ski Instructor of America (PSIA) training course, had taken a spill and was hit on that calf with one of my skis.

The big ugly welt had come and gone, but it seems the blow had damaged the vein.

I was in the hospital for about ten days, the first five or six with my foot up on a Heparin drip to prevent future blood clots. Following protocol, I was then placed on Coumadin tablets; Coumadin is a brand name for Warfarin Sodium; it's also used as rat poison! When you're on this stuff, the clotting time of your blood has to be monitored closely. Too little is not therapeutic, too much can cause bleeding and strokes. I would be on the stuff and grounded for six months; the FAA doesn't allow you to fly while on Coumadin.

A Major American Scandal

My six-month hiatus from USAir on medical leave was kind of primer for retirement six years later and also a mixed bag of emotions. Although I missed flying, there were many things to do and no excuse not to do them. During the time off, I spent a lot of effort helping to launch the Professional Pilots Federation, a task that was both time consuming and challenging. I served as vice president of the PPF from the time of its inception in early 1991 until 1998.

As I have said, PPF has only one mission, the elimination or amendment of the Age 60 Rule. The Age 60 Rule, FAR 121.383(3), prohibits a pilot from operating an airplane beyond his or her sixtieth birthday under Part 121 of the Federal Air Regulations—that section governing scheduled air carriers. The rule is blatant discrimination against professional airline pilots. Consider, at age 60 all FAA issued pilot licenses and all other ratings, including that of an Airline Transport Pilot remain valid. There is also no age limit to holding a FAA Class I medical certificate, which is the highest medical standard required for airline captains. While prohibited from serving as a pilot on a U.S. scheduled airliner, you still have the privileges of the licenses you hold and can fly the same airplanes in nonscheduled commercial activity, those not covered by Part 121. For example, test pilots for Boeing can and do fly over the age of 60.

The story behind the Age 60 Rule is one of America's greatest scandals. In 1958, President Dwight Eisenhower appointed General

Elwood (Pete) Quesada as the first administrator of the newly formed
FAA. Gen. Quesada had commanded the Tactical Air Forces in the
European Theater under Eisenhower during World War II. C.R.
Smith, then CEO of American Airlines, was Quesada's personal
friend and had also been an Air Corps general in World War II.

C.R. Smith was engaged in a bitter dispute with his pilots over
his belief that they should be forced to retire at age 60. American
was receiving the first of its Boeing 707 fleet and he thought the
older guys would cost too much to train. Back then all training was
done in the aircraft; there were no simulators and in-flight training
was expensive. Smith's assumptions proved to be untrue and were
based purely on his opinion. Also in 1958, a few pilots forced to retire
at TWA and Western at age 60 were reinstated through arbitration
under the Railway Labor Act. Smith had a dilemma. He was locked
in bitter contract negotiations with the pilots, forced retirement as
a key issue, and the pilots were being upheld under the RLA. He
needed help from friends in high places, and what better friend than
"Pete" Quesada, the new Administrator of the FAA?

On February 5, 1959, Smith sent a personal letter to Quesada
acknowledging the arbitration loss of the age 60-retirement issues and
seeking from the FAA a regulation to fix his labor problem. The letter
is public information obtained under the Freedom Of Information
Act. I feel certain that if FOYA had existed in 1959 (it was enacted
in 1966) that letter would have been destroyed and never seen again.
Unhindered by the FAA's lack of congressional authority to interfere
in labor issues, Quesada forged ahead to promulgate the Age 60
Rule in December 1959. It was done without a shred of supporting
scientific data. Immediately following, and upholding a mockery of
due process, a Federal District Court refused to enjoin enforcement
of the Age 60 Rule, citing Quesada's wartime record. The die was
cast. In America, the emperor's enforcers could do no wrong—
particularly under the guise of air safety.

Quesada (the war hero) retired from the FAA after a few
lackluster years and was immediately elected to American Airline's
Board of Directors in January 1961. Reward for services rendered?
I think so. Subsequent laws for retired federal officials would have

made it illegal. But this was 1961, and many of the safeguards we have now did not exist.

Ironically, at the same time I was hired by Mohawk Airlines on November 2, 1959, General Quesada had already planned my forced retirement on the day of my sixtieth birthday—thanks Pete! My munificent government would never, however, get around to providing Social Security benefits to airline pilots at age 60; in fact, the age for full benefits would be increased from age 65 to 67. Of course, back in my early twenties the thought of turning 60 seemed light years away. Yet I was deeply offended that my government would ruthlessly discriminate against my profession. During the 1960s, ALPA half-heartedly opposed the rule, but in my union work at Mohawk I wasn't directly involved beyond voicing support to overturn the rule. Mohawk was still a young airline.

****

Jumping ahead to the 1980s, still caring and interested, I was a financial contributor to a group of about 100 other pilots supporting a few petitioners (Baker, Aman and others) for exemption from the rule. They petitioned to be exempted on the basis of additional medical testing and scrutiny as a limited test group. The law firm of Bell, Boyd & Lloyd, specializing in labor issues, with headquarters in Washington and Chicago, represented them. I got to know the lead assigned attorney, Alan Serwer, fairly well.

On a related issue, Alan used me as an expert witness on behalf of a group of American Airlines pilots suing American for refusing access to the flight engineer's seat to pilots over 60. Flight engineers are not restricted by the Age 60 Rule. My expertise was being a USAir check pilot on the 727; USAir had a large group of flight engineers over age 60 who had bid down from captain to the engineer's seat on the 72 rather than retire. I testified that those at USAir were an asset to safety, and answered related questions.

The Baker/Aman petition was ultimately lost in the Federal Appellant Court for the 7th Circuit in 1990—the American flight engineer case is still in litigation fifteen years later. Don't let anybody fool you: Justice in America is for those who can afford it. These two cases alone have cost hundreds of thousands of dollars in legal fees.

With Baker/Aman lost, many of us wanted to continue the fight, but we had no organization; we had simply sent money to the law firm to cover legal fees. In early 1991, after many telephone calls crisscrossing the country, Chuck Nyren (Delta) called together a steering committee to consider the formation of such an organization. The meeting was held at a Washington D.C. hotel. Those whom I remember attending were Sam Woolsey (United), Carroll Fitzgerald (FedEx), Fred Arnt (American), Bill Reiners (American), Bert Yetman (Southwest), myself (USAir) and three or four others.

Fortunately, Bill Reiners had brought a friend who was an organizational whiz and he kept the group on point. Bit by bit, the organization took form.

We gave ourselves a name, the Professional Pilots Federation (PPF). Our goal was to have board members from all the nation's airlines, much like ALPA. To start, the representatives of each airline present selected a member of the PPF Board of Directors. Chuck Nyren was elected chairman of the board. The board then elected PPF's operating officers; Bert Yetman was elected president; I was named vice president and Bill Reiners secretary/treasurer. All the officers were also members of the board of directors. The BOD and the officers would be volunteers and receive no pay or other compensation.

To avoid the appearance of a labor union, our mission statement needed to be clear, concise and singular. It is simply "to eliminate or amend the Age 60 Rule."

Everyone recognized that a great deal of time and effort would need to be spent on a membership drive and fund-raising. PPF would also have to actively lobby Congress and try to establish better relationships with the White House, the FAA, airline managements and those pilots' unions not openly hostile to a rule change, as were ALPA and APA.

PPF in time would need to mount another legal petition, but with a different strategy. In Baker/Aman, we petitioned for exemption rather than for repeal of the Age 60 Rule. That decision had been made to placate the unions and the airlines and to offer up to the FAA a limited group of those willing to undergo vigorous additional testing. It didn't work. The opposition wasn't going to allow even modest relief to senior pilots.

That's where it stood when we left Washington after that first meeting, lots to do and no road maps. While still in the hospital recovering from the phlebitis episode, I passed the time filling legal pads with ideas and strategy suggestions. Bill Reiners and I grew to be close friends; we still keep in touch fourteen years later. Coming from a similar background as union reps, we understood how the unions worked and were capable of opposing them on age 60 while keeping a sense of balance. Bert was a retired Air Force fighter pilot. Southwest Airlines was a second career. He was deeply conservative and we often didn't hear the same music. But he was strongly committed to overturning the Age 60 Rule and remains president of the PPF to this day (summer, 2003).

Shortly after PPF was incorporated, we retained Sparkman and Cole, a Washington lobbying firm that had been recommended. Dean Sparkman seemed to know everyone in D.C. and Tim Cole was a former deputy administrator of the FAA. That was the beginning of my political education. They opened a lot of doors and we spent a great deal of time together in the halls of Congress. Tim Cole carried on as our federal access after Dean left Washington to do other things.

For a short time we retained a marketing firm to send bulk mailings to airline pilots to recruit members and solicit contributions. The numbers just weren't there to justify the cost and after a few months we had to let them go. Early on we got most of our members by word of mouth. As we learned, and I guess should have expected from human nature, pilots wouldn't focus on their forced retirement until they started counting the months down to their own professional demise. In the time I served, there were some highly active members from most of the airlines in the country and even some from overseas. Finding a law firm to represent us and develop a different approach took months. Opposing a government agency like the FAA can be a tremendous amount of work that could bury a small law office under mountains of paper. PPF also had limited resources and would have to assess its membership to pay the legal fees. We appealed to some of the big names in that sort of litigation to take us on pro bono, with no luck. After several zigzags, we lucked out in finding Mike Pangia and Nick Cobbs who shared law offices in Washington.

Mike had been a head litigator for the FAA before going into private practice and he became highly sought after to represent victims of major aviation accidents. He was also a commercial pilot and owned and flew a SNJ, a WWII primary training aircraft in original Navy markings. He came from Long Island and had learned to fly at Zahn's Airport many years after I had instructed there. Nick had an aviation related background in maritime law and worked on certain cases with Mike. Nick would do most of the up-front work with Mike in support. Mike didn't work pro bono, but he billed us for only a fraction of his time. Although it took some time, PPF developed into a splendid dedicated working group. For all of us, Age 60 became less about keeping our jobs and much more an important civil rights fight. I read and became a student of discrimination. My studies confirmed what I felt; it is a terrible thing. To be subjected to it is to be made less human. A black person cannot be white, a woman cannot be man, and on and on as societies throughout history have dehumanized and outcast others. The motives are always the same, either fear or greed. What was keeping Age 60 in place was a combination of both.

ALPA and APA, the major pilots' unions, stopped opposing the Age 60 Rule as their demographics changed and more and more junior pilots coveted the senior jobs. This was exacerbated by deregulation, which forced so many pilots to the bottom of new seniority lists. Changes in the IRS Code also limited the maximum amount of money that could be taken out of a qualified pension plan. The IRS uses a formula based upon Social Security's normal retirement age; if the benefit is taken at a younger age, the qualified amount goes down. You still get the money either way, but it is taxed immediately as normal income. Because of the Age 60 Rule, the unions were successful in getting Congress to reduce that age for airline pilots to 60.

Make no mistake, promotional opportunities and tax advantages are important considerations for any professional person. But are they valid reasons for a labor union to foster age discrimination? No, they are not. Discrimination breaks labor's most important covenant—unity above all. Only with unity can labor stand against the rape of workers in a "deregulated" environment and only with unity can pension plans be protected. As union officials caved in to the greedy young Turks, the future of the airline pilots' profession, including all the negotiated pension plans, was in serious jeopardy. And guess what? The old horses that they so vigorously put out to pasture had negotiated those contracts and could have been their best allies.

As I have noted, in 2003 every major airline in the country is in financial trouble and either close to or in bankruptcy. Pension plans have been terminated and benefits made dependent on the Pension Benefit Guarantee Corporation (PBGC), a quasi-government safety net. At best, those pilots affected will only receive partial retirement benefits.

In 1968, Congress passed the Age Discrimination in Employment Act (ADEA), which made age discrimination in employment illegal. Responsibility of administering the act was given to the Secretary of Labor. The secretary, at the request of the FAA, immediately declared the Age 60 Rule to be a Bona Fide Occupational Qualification (BFOQ). Ah, the power of government. Congress amended the ADEA in 1979, creating the Equal Employment Opportunities Commission (EEOC) as a blanket overseer of discrimination laws, including the ADEA. In 1981, the EEOC rescinded the Department of Labor's declaration of the Age 60 Rule as a BFOQ. The EEOC became our ally in the Age 60 battle but didn't have the authority to fight a federal agency.

****

Our efforts to lobby Congress and the FAA never produced more than perfunctory results. The politicians, ever mindful of the next campaign and how to finance it, were not willing to get on the wrong side of the AFL-CIO. And the FAA, with its dual mandate of safety and promotion of the airline industry, wasn't going to oppose those who held their agency's purse strings. Screw the senior pilots. We weren't a large voting block, nor were we able to contribute large sums to political campaigns.

Under the direction of Tim Cole, we had twenty or thirty pilots in uniform beating on the doors of their representatives and senators. On one of those missions, Bill Reiners and I were waiting for an elevator in a Senate office building when Senator Edward Kennedy came up beside us to wait for the Senators Only elevator. He invited us to join him when his elevator came first and he asked what brought us to town. We explained and he laughed and said he was running for reelection and hoped to save his job too!

What the FAA did in the Baker/Aman petition was dismiss out of hand our expert medical testimony and the protocols those experts had developed, and hold petitioners to a standard higher than any other required by the FAA—one hundred percent reliability. Every part and every system on an aircraft has a statistical "failure" rate. It could be one in a million or one in five million, but everyone knows that equipment fails. That's why we have multi-engine airliners with backup systems.

The redundancy for the flight deck is a two pilot crew, with each pilot held to a high medical standard. The captain is required to pass a strict FAA Class 1 medical examination every six months, the first officer once a year. In my airline career, I underwent such testing the better part of eighty times. It is a thorough physical that includes disclosure of your current medical history, electrocardiogram, vision, auditory and neurological testing and a subjective analysis by the flight surgeon. Short of being an astronaut or a military pilot, no other cohort of human beings undergoes such stringent routine testing.

The system works. There has not been a single accident attributed to the death or incapacitation of a pilot in scheduled airline service. A few pilots have died in flight and many more have taken ill, usually from food poisoning. In all instances, the remaining pilot landed the aircraft safely. Pilots are now prohibited from eating the same crew meals.

All this was known when the FAA argued before the 7th Circuit Court that the agency could not protect the traveling public if airline pilots flew beyond the age of 60. The agency went so far as to misrepresent an accountant as a statistician, who used useless data from the medical records of private pilots. Although two of the three justices upheld the FAA as the "expert" agency, the court severely criticized the FAA for its lack of sound scientific data.

Because of that admonishment from the 7th Circuit Court, the FAA launched the Hilton study, also referred to as the Civil Aero Medical Institute (CAMI) report. The PPF had no choice but to wait for the findings of the study before initiating a further action.

In early 1993, the FAA released the findings of the Hilton study, which were highly favorable to our cause. The study found "no hint of an increase in accident rates as pilots near age 60" and concluded that the retirement age may be safely raised. This was good news and we were guardedly optimistic when the FAA scheduled a half-day public meeting to gather comments on the Hilton study and the Age 60 Rule.

The public meeting drew such an overwhelming response that it lasted two days with 83 percent of those who testified speaking against the rule. Bert Yetman spoke eloquently for PPF and we presented a host of other speakers. One was David Cronin, the captain of United flight 811, who had done such a marvelous job bringing that ill-fated Boeing 747 back to Honolulu after an explosive decompression that severely damaged the aircraft. David was forced to retire, against his wishes, just a few weeks after the incident. His story of that flight ran chills down your spine.

Another PPF member who spoke was a black American Airlines captain who shared his experience as a U.S. Air Force pilot deployed to the southern United States. He had been forced to separate from his crew at a hotel that wouldn't rent him a room because he was black. Now he told the audience filling the room that he was being discriminated again because of his age. There were a lot of moist eyes. Later that evening when Bill Reiners and I spoke of him, Bill openly cried and I couldn't have loved him more for it.

Representatives from foreign airlines also spoke passionately against the rule. They wanted relief so that their older pilots could fly into the United States. Some countries, including Iceland, had waivers to do so. Israel particularly needed to retain its older pilots. Subsequently, at our suggestion, we were told Israeli captains over age 60 flying into the United States would temporarily transfer command to the younger first officer. What the heck, the ICAO rule only prohibits the pilot-in-command from being over 60. Stupid rules warrant innovative solutions. The first officer knew who the boss was if he ever wanted to return home.

Perhaps the most significant appearance at the public meeting was by representatives of the Joint Aviation Authority. JAA was in the process of combining the national aviation authorities within the newly created European Union. They had done a lot of work on Age 60 and were preparing to raise the age in Europe. In simple terms, what they did was to analyze mortality rates for the general population of people 60 and 65, and based on that and other medical statistics were able to conclude there was no substantial difference. Pilots also would have undergone vigorous medical examinations for many years, eliminating those who developed debilitating illnesses along the way. The survivors would form an even safer cohort.

ALPA and APA also had spokespersons. The ALPA pilot, who was chairman of their medical subcommittee, explained that the vigorousness of airline operations would simply be too much for a 60-year-old. Fifty-nine is okay, but over 60 would be asking too much. That was the extent of ALPA and APA's scientific presentation. I was shocked when from the mouth of Rod Neibauer, my longtime friend sitting in front of me came a resoundingly loud "wimp." Rod is a full-time, 100 percent gentleman, but he just couldn't stand the drivel and be silent. I could have kissed him.

Did all this sway the FAA? Not at all. Age 60 was a political mandate having nothing to do with safety. Instead the FAA exercised its imperial power and returned the Hilton study to its authors, instructing them to come up with "an age—any age." Not surprisingly, using a bazaar risk analysis protocol, they found their boss, the FAA, to be exactly correct—age 60 was indeed the right number!

PPF was well prepared. Immediately following the hearing in 1993, Nick Cobbs and Mike Pangia filed two comprehensive petitions with the FAA on our behalf. The major petition would eliminate or amend the rule—the second would give U.S. airline pilots rights equal to foreign pilots, one pilot other than the pilot in command would be permitted to be over age 60. It took the FAA more than two years to render a decision.

During that time, we actively lobbied anyone in Congress or the Clinton administration who would listen to us. One meeting, behind closed doors, I'll never forget. Tim Cole and Mike Pangia had arranged a meeting with the general council of the Department of Transportation. DOT would call the shots on our petitions, not David Hinson, the lower level administrator of the FAA. The secretary of the DOT at the time was Federico Peña, also known as the Teflon Cabinet Official. President Clinton, wishing his cabinet to look like America, gave us a Hispanic secretary. Never mind that he knew nothing of planes, trains and automobiles; he was a former mayor of Denver. What Secretary Peña knew was where his political bread and butter came from.

What Peña's general council said made me sick. I'm the son of immigrants, brought up feeling that my country, America, stood for what was right. I'm not naive. I know that what's right can be subjective but, still, Americans often make the effort and strive to do what is right. At least I hope that's true. But the message we got was loud and clear: Forget it. The White House was committed to upholding ALPA and the AFL-CIO on Age 60—end of discussion. Right or wrong be damned, campaign money and political support were on the table.

Secretary Peña fell from grace for allowing safety infractions to be covered up by the FAA following the crash of a ValuJet DC-9 into the Florida Everglades on May 11,1996, which killed 110 people. Within months, President Clinton moved him over to be Secretary of the Department of Energy, where he lasted only a year. We caught a break in May 1995, when Australia dropped the Age 60 Rule. Australian Chief Justice Wilcox ruled: "Given the time and effort expended in America examining the age 60 rule, it is remarkable to say so, but it seems to me that none of the cited studies supports any conclusion about the relationship between that rule and aircraft safety."

In December 1995, with Randy Babbitt, the president of ALPA, at his side, Secretary Peña announced the denial of our petitions and expanded the Age 60 Rule to cover pilots flying commuter type aircraft with ten seats or more. Pilots over 60 had been flying commuters for years with no problem whatsoever.

After our closed door meeting with Peña's general council, we weren't surprised by the DOT ruling, but we were shocked nonetheless that our government would put yet another group of competent pilots out of work. The next day the PPF filed for review of the FAA's actions in the D.C. Court of Appeals.

During the following summer, in June, the Joint Aviation Authority officially changed the retirement age for pilots to 65. Twelve nations in the European Union were affected then, more are now. But they still cannot fly to the United States as pilots in command.

Concurrent with the JAA announcement, the U.S. Court of Appeals in Washington heard oral arguments in open court. Nike Cobbs, tuned like a fine piano, made our argument, with Mike Pangia at his table. We filled the courtroom with about two hundred airline pilots in uniform. It was quite a sight! Well instructed, the pilots didn't make a sound, just listened. A year later, the court issued a two-to-one denial. In her dissenting opinion, Judge Patricia Wald, wrote: "More importantly, the Age 60 Rule stands as an instance of government-mandated age discrimination for a particular group of employees." We immediately filed for a rehearing before the Court En Banc—the entire Court, not just the three justices. We were refused. The following February, PPF filed for U.S. Supreme Court certiorari, but the Supreme Court declined to hear the case.

By this time I had been forced to retire and, although still committed to the issue, was in disagreement with the PPF Board of Directors as to the best strategy upon which to proceed. I would have petitioned to specifically raise the age to 63 or 65, based upon the regulation for Western Europe. Most of the board and many of our key supporters were already over 60, as I was, and would not be young enough to benefit from an age increase. They felt that they needed nothing less than the elimination of the rule or an exemption. It was time for me to move on with my life and make room for new blood at PPF.

PPF went through another petition and appeal process for exemption, with even more medical evidence and better protocols, but it was denied by the FAA and again the PPF lost in court. Now I read that they are trying again, but plan to base the appeal on FAA fraud—a long shot that literally accuses the agency of a deliberate criminal act. I truly wish them the best of luck.

Unfortunately, the alliance of our government and labor unions in disregarding civil rights has made the profession of being an airline pilot not very desirable. Greed is like a cancer eating away at America.

Last Landing at Logan

After that final flight to Frankfurt and our last evening out in Wiesbaden, I had a good night's sleep and woke up on the eve of my sixtieth birthday. True to routine, a copy of the *International Herald Tribune* in hand, I was at the hotel restaurant when it opened. Sue passed, opting for the extra hour's rest and coffee and pastry delivered by me. The Crowne Plaza restaurant served the best German breakfast buffet you can imagine: smoked salmon, herring, cheeses of every kind, dark bread and rolls, fresh fruit—a true feast. At 2 a.m. East Coast time, I always thought it a great way to start the day. There were more good wishes from crew members checking in as our crew was assembling, checking out and waiting for our crew bus. The inbound had arrived on time and it looked good for an on-time departure for our flight home as 817.

The contracted bus service usually provided full-sized Mercedes tour buses that were really plush, but on occasion would substitute two minivans. We got one of the regular buses for this trip, but some of the minivan rides were memorable. The German autobahns are not for the timid. Even so, some of those minivan drivers really pushed the envelope.

US Airways shared flight operation at Frankfurt with British Airways. They were mostly German nationals who were highly professional and did a great job. Over time I got to know them and they knew they could count on me to help them in any way that I could. An

197

aloof or uncooperative captain could screw up an on-time departure in countless ways and imprecise flight planning would sacrifice revenue. Flights from Frankfurt west were always up to maximum gross takeoff weights because of the extra fuel needed to counter the prevailing easterly jet streams. US Airways computerized weight and balance system limited the gate release weight to 351,000 pounds, the maximum certified gross takeoff weight. The computer simply didn't understand that the maximum certified taxi weight is 352,200 pounds and that the additional 1,200 pounds is always burned off taxiing out to the runway. That additional weight could translate to six or seven passengers or revenue freight being left behind. The only one with the authority to override the computer was the captain and I did it routinely.

The bottom line is that by doing my job properly I enabled others to do theirs. That's the kind of captains I tried to train as a line captain and for a while as a line instructor/check airman. As was taught to me, authority must be coupled with responsibility and leadership to be successful. At any rate, the guys at operations were very thoughtful. I wound up with a basket of trinkets and memorabilia, but had no idea what else the station manager had up his sleeve. I would find out soon enough.

In the meantime, cabin crewmembers had their own ideas. The flight was full and I know those passengers didn't have any idea in the world what they were in for. The crew had prepared for a party across the Atlantic: papier-mâché, cake, the whole works.

Now you have to understand that a pilot is only as good as his last landing. Last flight or no, it would be safe and professionally conducted. The cockpit routine was done by the book, except that I asked Larry, the first officer, to handle the PA welcome aboard and so forth. He needless to say mentioned the significance of the flight. Fortunately, nobody asked to get off!

I thought it was sweet that the station manager personally gave the wave off salute, although I thought his grin was a little shit-eating. I would soon learn why. As we turned down the taxiway toward runway 07L, the ground controller asked us to deviate to a parallel taxiway, and then politely suggested that the Frankfurt

Airport Fire and Rescue Crew would like to salute the captain. Up came fire engines abreast of the aircraft on both sides of the taxiway; out came a bridge of water over the aircraft. Somewhat further down was the commander standing at attention with a dress salute.

Now you have to understand: I was commanding a U.S. flag carrier at Frankfurt, Germany. Such a tribute had never been given before.

Abeam of the fire chief, I stopped the aircraft and with tears in my eyes returned a military salute that General Patton would have been proud of. Wow! It is a memory I will always cherish. Thank God for Larry. I asked him to assure the passengers that we weren't on fire and tell them what had occurred. I sure couldn't have done it right then.

****

Frankfurt/Main Airport has three runways, all 13,123 feet long, two parallel runways, 07L/25R and 07R/25L and a north/south runway. The airport elevation is 364 feet above sea level. Frankfurt is without question one of the world's best airports and particularly well suited for large jet aircraft.

Our takeoff weight was right up to maximum at 351,000 pounds; the reference takeoff speeds for 10 of flap were V1 160 knots, Vr 164K, V2 168K. Let me tell you, that long runway is really nice to have in front of you at those speeds. A stop from the go/no go decision speed (V1) of 160K at that weight would be a maximum breaking effort that would leave the two trucks of four wheels of the landing gear glowing red hot. After a high-speed stop it would take hours for the brakes to cool sufficiently to meet criteria for another takeoff.

Hot brakes and wheels are extremely dangerous. Ground personnel have been killed when smoking glowing wheels were unadvisedly hit with a fire-extinguishing agent, causing an explosion. Braking is friction, the transfer of kinetic energy into heat. All modern big airplanes have antiskid breaking protection. A locked wheel would immediately blow out; before the advent of good antiskid systems they did regularly.

The ability to deflect jet thrust forward also offers an increased safety margin, but it is not used to set the criteria for determining performance. The engines do not really reverse, but rather deflectors are mechanically put into the engine's fan air. On the 76s with GE engines they are powered pneumatically; on the Pratt & Whitney configuration they are powered hydraulically. While both have safeguards that prevent reverse thrust from being used in flight, the hydraulically powered Pratt & Whitney version was found responsible for a deployment at high speed in flight, creating a yaw that caused the vertical stabilizer of a Lauda charter flight to fail, dooming all on board. The pneumatic power on the GEs is not powerful enough to deploy the deflectors at high speed.

With the before takeoff checklist completed, Larry made the standard PA announcement that we had been cleared for takeoff so the flight attendants could get seated, and I took the runway for the last time in my career.

I had come the full circle from always being too young to mandatory forced retirement at age 60. You had to be 16 to solo, that's when I soloed; 17 for a private pilot's license, that's when I got it; 18 for a commercial pilot's license, that's when I got it, along with an instructor's certificate and an instrument rating. As I recounted earlier, it took me several years to land an airline job because I was too young. In my second year with Mohawk Airlines I got an Airline Transport Rating (ATR) at age 23, the minimum age, and began flying as the youngest captain in the industry.

You could call that takeoff from Frankfurt normal except that all takeoffs are unique and special. As we have seen, an aircraft on the ground is like a fish out of water; it is clumsy, slow and awkward. Once in flight, an airplane is in its element and a thing of beauty. Each takeoff is like a rebirth and always with the knowledge that, however long the flight, a landing must follow.

The standard instrument departure (SID) off of 7L call for flying runway heading to 800 feet, then a left turn around the city of Frankfurt and leveling at 5,000 feet so as to pass under arrivals. Departure control radar would take you north far away from the airport traffic before swinging you northwest on course and allowing a climb. In the United States, all flights under 10,000 feet must restrict speed to under 250 knots; Germany permits a faster speed at the discretion of the controller, which was often allowed. Let me tell you, it's a blast to motor along at 350 knots, over 400 statute miles per hour, in a large aircraft at low altitude.

The weather was good, allowing a nice view of the Rhine River passing Cologne and Dusseldorf. Our route would take us abeam of Amsterdam and on up over Scotland to join the NAT track great circle route planned.

Above 18,000 feet, flights going east are at odd altitudes, FL 350, 370, and so forth. West is at even altitudes FL 360, 380 and such. At high altitude, a 76 burns about 10,000 pounds of fuel per hour, much more at climb power or at low altitude. Jet fuel weighs about seven pounds per gallon, gasoline about six and water eight. The goal would be to reach as high an altitude as possible at the NAT track gateway for fuel conservation during the ocean crossing. This was limited by the weight of the aircraft due to the low and high-speed buffet margin. To allow a climb to FL 360 at the gateway, the aircraft could weigh no more than 320,000 pounds, down from 351,000 at takeoff, a fuel burn of 31,000 pounds.

Though the Earth's atmosphere extends 1,500 miles above the surface, 75 percent of it is below 10 miles or FL 600. From the surface to seven miles (420) is called the troposphere; it varies from five miles (300) at the Earth's poles to 10 miles thick at the equator. Above that is the stratosphere, which extends up to 30 miles (900). The ozone layer that protects us from harmful ultraviolet rays—the layer that modern humankind is destroying with pollution—is located in the stratosphere between 10 to 30 miles above the surface. It is in the lower stratosphere between 300 and 400 that subsonic (below the speed of sound) jets operate most efficiently. Supersonic jets such as the Concord and military aircraft like to get up higher, although I don't think any operate routinely above 600.

It is a hostile environment. Barometric air pressure drops from the sea level average of 14.7 pounds per square inch, which is equal to 29.92 inches of mercury down to 5.56 inches of mercury at 400, where the outside air temperature is normally about -50C (centigrade). Interestingly, from that point the temperature rises back up to about 00C at the top of the stratosphere. But then the temperature drops like a stone to about 80C between 32 miles and 52 miles in what is called the mesosphere. Then in the ionosphere, which is part of the thermosphere, extending up to 435 miles, the temperature rises to 100C.

To create a livable cabin, the 76 and other jet airliners bleed off a stage of engine compression prior to fuel combustion and meter that hot compressed air through cooling units into the cabin. Uncooled, that bled air would cook everyone as if they were in a convection oven. It's like blowing up a balloon. The maximum cabin pressure on the 76 is 8.6 pounds per square inch, enough to maintain a cabin pressure of about 8,000 feet at the maximum cruise altitude of 430.

Passengers would be comforted to know, as they sit enjoying the show and a cocktail, that a rapid decompression that could be caused by a blown hatch or a turbine blade lunged through the fuselage by a blown engine, or a small bomb, or even a pistol shot in a critical place would immediately plunge the cabin into a dense ice fog at a temperature of -50C. The drop in air pressure would suck all the air out of your lungs and unless you don the drop-down mask— which you probably can't see—you'll be unconscious in a matter of seconds.

Not to worry, however, pilots train in the simulator (sim) for rapid decompression. Up front, we have quick donning oxygen masks and above 410 one pilot is required to wear it at all times. Above 250, if one pilot leaves the seat the remaining pilot must put it on. The drill is kind of fun. It is accompanied by a simulated loud air noise that the sim performs exactly like the real aircraft. The idea is to get down from high altitude to a breathable 10,000 feet. From 430, that's a high dive of 33,000 feet. About the fastest a 76 can come down without exceeding its maximum structural speed is 5,000 feet a minute, a dive lasting over six minutes. Also, if the decompression was the result of structural damage, not just a failure of the pressurization system, the decision might be made to descend at a slower speed to avoid stress.

I have no doubt that there would be passenger fatalities with a rapid decompression at high altitude. There have even been deaths attributed to loss of cabin pressure in private jets as the crew lost consciousness and the airplane flew on autopilot until running out of fuel.

The paradox of a subsonic aircraft is that at high altitude the envelope between flying too slow and stalling and flying too fast into high-speed buffet, which is the onset of loss of control due to compression as parts of the aircraft exceed the sound barrier. This is affectionately called the coffin corner. A 76 weighing 280,000 pounds at 410 has to operate at an indicated airspeed between 212-235 knots. The aircraft is actually going a whole lot faster, but the indicated airspeed and the lift capacity of the wings are a function of air density. That's a mighty skinny margin, particularly if there's clear air turbulence that increases gravity forces, which increase the stall speed. The loss of an engine at that altitude would require an immediate drift down to 270.

Not too many years ago, a Japan Airlines B-747 lost an engine at high altitude and it went unnoticed. The airspeed diminished, causing a stall and down she went for thousands of feet until the crew regained control. Fortunately, they made it to San Francisco after incurring major damage.

So relax and enjoy the flight.

All that said, the ability of the 76 to operate at relatively high weights at the top end of the NAT track altitudes was a great advantage, both for fuel efficiency and passenger comfort. Aircraft like the Boeing 747, the DC-10 and Lockheed 1011 would be below us most of the time, bouncing around in the cloud tops. Of course then there was the occasional Concord well above us and going about twice as fast at supersonic speed. If they were relatively close by, we experienced their shock wave, or sonic boom.

Flight 817 left Frankfurt on time at 10:40 (04:40 Boston time), and was scheduled to arrive at Boston at 13:00, eight hours and twenty minutes later. The sun would only gain two hours on us over an eight-hour period. Consequently, the sun was always in your eyes. Boeing provided transparent sun visors that, like the visors in your car, never seemed to be in the right place, so good sunglasses were a must. Some captains would block the windows with charts or newspapers but that always made me uncomfortable. Then to the rescue came "Toys-R-Us" with a great product to screen sunlight from children in cars—a sheet of dark transparent soft film that stuck to the window. That worked great and everybody had a sheet.

There are several health risks involved as well. Unprotected eyes would literally sunburn and cause cataracts. The unprotected face and arms would be subjected to higher levels of ultraviolet light, increasing the risk of skin cancer. The cabin pressurization and air-conditioning had its own problems. Although the cabin altitude would be kept below 8,000 feet, which is still high enough to cause some oxygen depravation and the lower pressure to cause the body to bloat and retain water.

Heart patients and those with pulmonary problems are wise to check with their doctors before flying long range, high altitude flights. With prior notice, the airlines will provide portable oxygen. A typical scenario would be for a passenger to have breakfast, maybe a Bloody Mary or two, take a snooze, and then get up to go to the lavatory, only to feel faint and keel over. Usually simply elevating that person's feet gets more oxygen to the brain and he or she feels okay to continue. If not, flights have to divert.

I know when I returned home after an overseas trip I weighed several pounds more. The extra weight would drop as my body got back to normal and lost water. Cabin attendants complained of legs swelling; they all wore support hose. They claimed that they would gain a dress size until the water loss kicked in. I don't think the body particularly likes being blown up and deflated and that doing so routinely poses a health hazard.

The B-767 and other airliners recirculate about 50 percent of the cabin air to conserve fuel. This reduces the volume of engine bypass air being plumbed into the cabin and reduces fuel consumption slightly from only allowing fresh air in and exhausting. For smoke removal, that option is there and I did so periodically to clear the air, particularly before smoking was banned on international flights. The manufacturers and the government continue to assure us that ultraviolet light at high altitude is not a problem, that the cabin pressure envelope is okay and that bacteria and other microbes are filtered out and present no health problems. I think they are wrong on all counts and venture to guess that if accurate data is ever kept it will be proven.

Unlike the eastbound night flights, when the night sky and the dawn could be breathtaking, daylight westbound flights featured the Earth visible below. Every flight over Europe was a history lesson. How could you not think of the dark ages, the crusades, the renaissance or the world wars? I often thought of the tremendous loss of life of allied heavy bombers in World War II, the B-17s, B-24s and Lancasters, which were sitting ducks.

The ocean itself was always different. The North Sea was perpetually rough and dotted with oil rigs, the North Atlantic rarely without whitecaps and changing wind directions. I always marveled to think of the courage and skill of early mariners. And the guts of the Merchant Marine, which suffered monstrous loses at the hands of German submarine wolf packs to keep supplies going to England and Russia.

Extended over-water two-engine aircraft were a relatively new thing made possible by the advent of huge, reliable jet engines. Each engine on the 76 is equal in thrust to all four of the early engines on the B-707 and DC-8. But a B-707 or a DC-8 can fly just fine with the loss of one engine and still limp along and maintain flight with the loss of two. The big twins can fly fine with the loss of an engine, but if we lost two we became a huge glider. There's a difference.

To make over-water flight as safe as possible for the big twins, there is a lot of redundancy, along with other safeguards. If an airline's engine reliability statistics were to show signs of weakness, its extended over-water certification would be yanked in a heartbeat. The proof is in the pudding, though: No large twin has ever been lost due to extended over-water operations.

But over-water flight does keep you on your toes. For instance, there are procedures for ditching at sea and circumstances that could warrant doing so. That one in million chance of a multiple engine failure is one; an uncontrollable fire is another. Big aircraft have successfully ditched at sea. We had every known incident discussed in training, along with the unsuccessful cases. There is also a lot of film documentation.

The procedure was to land while you still had power, at a minimum rate of descent above stalling speed. It was to be done with the landing gear up and landing flaps with the sea swells. The engineers assured us that the under wing engines would shear off before the wings failed; of course no one ever tried to find out.

Each of the four doors, two up front and two in the back, is equipped with dual lane pneumatic escape slide/rafts that automatically deploy and inflate when the door is opened. The deal is that you can move from the aircraft to the raft without getting your feet wet. Each raft has a capacity of 58, with an overload capacity of 78.

In good humor, I've seen countless full airplanes disembark passengers at state of the art jet ways and always felt that was the most dangerous part of the flight. If by God's good grace we actually managed to fall into the sea without the aircraft disintegrating, getting 220 or more people into life rafts didn't seem highly probable. That thought always kept me alert over all that water.

To keep the odds in our favor, we always had an en route alternate within fuel capacity on one engine. On either side of the ocean, Gander (Newfoundland) and Shannon (Ireland) would be frequently used, with mid-point alternates at Sondre Stromfjord (Greenland), Keflavik (Iceland) and Lajies (Azores). In later years, we didn't use Sondre Stromfjord because it really is a tough airport with high terrain on three sides.

Usually Iceland was too far to the north of our route to see, which was the case on this flight. But we'd often fly over southern Greenland and did that day. The southern tip of Greenland is at N60.00 latitude and W45.00 longitude.

Early navigators could determine latitude pretty well from the position of the sun, but longitude was a lot harder unless you knew exactly what time it was. It was the advent of an accurate timepiece, or chronometer, that made accurate navigation possible. The world uses the time at 0 degrees longitude, which pass through Greenwich, England and is expressed as Greenwich mean time (GMT) for all navigation. The time is accurate to 0.001 of a second in 300 years with the use of atomic clocks that measure how atoms vibrate. The time is arrived at among nations and known as Universal Time.

Greenland is really fun to fly over. For starters, it's not green at all. Most of it is a compacted snow and ice plateau over ten thousand feet above sea level. The island is bordered on the east by the Denmark Strait and on the west by the Labrador Sea; Greenland is a possession of Denmark. On both sides massive ice flows down to the sea, launching equally massive icebergs.

It is an impressive sight that I always called to the attention of the passengers, with mixed results because all the window shades would be down and a movie playing. I always figured they could see the movie anytime; Greenland is another story.

The iceberg fields are really something. Seeing them makes you take the threat of global warming a lot more seriously. From a prospective five or six miles up, it is easy to see that if the ice caps start receding you'd better have a reservation on the ark.

Everybody knows that icebergs are serious business to shipping, especially those who saw the movie *Titanic*. The shipping lanes extend further south for that reason, but ship's captains like to take advantage of the ocean's currents and staying further north than the mid-Atlantic going to Europe is advantageous. In any case, the Titanic sank much closer to Newfoundland.

****

Somewhere along the line I was invited to the rear galley for a cake cutting ceremony. What a blast! The crew, with my wife in cahoots, had decorated the whole place with papier-mâché and a banner. Many of the passengers offered congratulations as I passed. Talk about icing on the cake!

Over my thirty-eight years with the airline, I had the privilege of flying with thousands of pilots and flight attendants. It is a special relationship, much like I think camaraderie in war would be. In truth, we were at war with the elements, to be sure, but also with a system that established the flight crew as the final arbiter of safety. From the time I started flying, many friends perished in the fight. I find myself thinking of people and events that happened thirty or forty years ago and realize that some of my friends have long passed on, but they still live in my memory.

So we all had a piece of cake and kept going on to Boston.

No matter how many times you cross the ocean, landfall is always a welcome event. It is also a busy time as control transfers from the NAT track system to the domestic radar controlled environment. Along with that comes a domestic routing that must be entered into the FMC and usually another step climb. In the days of reciprocating engines, it often meant a fuel stop at Gander or Goose Bay.

On some northern routings to Pittsburgh, we got an en route alternate of Kuujjuaq, Quebec, which is about 380 nautical miles northwest of Goose Bay. It is a small strip with only a 6,000-foot runway that has an interesting caution: Large animals in vicinity of airport. One day, just for fun, I called Kuujjuaq approach control and asked about the animals and what kind of overnight facilities they had for 222 people. The controller got a kick out of it, but as for facilities I think we would have been sleeping on board with an armed guard to keep the bears away.

The flight over Newfoundland is extremely interesting. There are countless lakes in a bleak forest. It is actually part of the boreal forest that circles the Earth's crown, extending across Canada, Alaska, Scandinavia and Siberia. Fashioned by arctic weather fronts, vanished glaciers and fire, it is truly bleak and inhabited by just a fraction of the life forms of warmer forests. From it comes lots of timber and in some places hydroelectric power, but most important to the creatures of the Earth, this vast area through photosynthesis filters out billions of tons of carbon dioxide and other greenhouse gases that affect weather and gives back our precious oxygen. This is increasingly important as tropical forests are being logged out of existence.

I wish all the world's political leaders were required to spend a week or two in Earth orbit. Perhaps the fragility of our home, Earth, would be better appreciated and the power of industry to consume our natural resources at Earth's peril kept in better balance. As it is now, money talks and the Earth walks.

As you fly further south, the terrain becomes lush when you fly over Nova Scotia and the coastline of Maine. The normal Boston arrival takes you somewhat offshore for a fuel-efficient high dive to Logan. The weather was clear with strong gusty winds; Logan was landing on runway 27 with departures on 22L and 22R. Runway 27 is 7,000 feet long, not that long for a 76. The approach takes you low abeam of the town of Winthrop and Dave Phipps's lovely home, which project right out into the bay.

Boy, I don't know how word travels, but Boston approach really had the welcome mat out. It's funny that over the years you get to recognize radio voices and style, people you never meet but have shared a professional life with.

The heat was on. I don't care how good you are, not every landing is a grease job and some, while safe, are not the ones you want to remember. Well, without false modesty, this one was a grease job and met with resounding applause from the cabin. Wow!

Not to be outdone by Frankfurt, Logan's fire department surrounded us on the ramp and provided another water halo. What a trip!

Parked at the gate, I completed the parking and securing checklist and repacked my flight kit for the last time, not to be opened again until I started work on this memoir five years later.

The welcoming committee on the jet way was sweet. The Boston mechanics who had met my flights for years were there, not only to do their job, which is to hear firsthand what condition the ship was in, but also to say farewell. That's no shit stuff. Some captains break balls, others know better. I always tried to be one of the latter. In turn, I could always count on them to be straight with me. I'm sure that not many passengers recognize the talent and hard work that the industry's mechanics and technicians do to make their flights safe. I do.

Waiting for the serious mechanical debriefing to be done was the Boston base chief pilot, Ed Schmidt. He had been promoted the year before from Captain Lou Kosakoski's base staff, after Lou succumbed to brain cancer. Ed is still Boston chief pilot as this is written. Lou was a great guy who had flown copilot for me when we were both based in New York. He and his wife were neighbors in Long Beach, a Long Island suburb not far from Kennedy International. Along with him were some of the base pilots and his secretary, who kept everyone's records straight. Pilots aren't great paper shufflers.

Joining them was Alice Carr, which was really a surprise. Alice worked with Tim Cole's Federal Access, the Washington lobbyists who had labored with me for years fighting the mandatory age 60-retirement rule.

The airport had a podium set up before a giant American flag in the terminal reception area. The pictures are fun to look back on.

I'm particularly pleased because, although I got a little misty eyed, I didn't altogether blow it. I think I could debate the devil, and I have fought the good fight often, yet those who have touched me with kindness know that I am a softy at heart.

Being before an American flag has a significance that goes back to Pan American, TWA, Pan Agra, Northwest and other pioneer flag carriers. In the early days, the flag on the side of an aircraft might well have been the only American presence in certain countries. The flag carriers of the United States truly have a proud heritage and I always felt a responsibility as the captain of a flagship overseas to live up to that tradition. Most people don't realize that perhaps today more than ever this represents our country's values possibly more than anything else. Terrorists know it. That's why we're their targets.

Next another cake, more good wishes, a few more pulls on the heartstrings and that was that. Do I miss the people, flying state of the art jet aircraft and the job? You bet I do. Am I pleased not to be flying today? Yes, because what a stupidly tragic place the airline industry has come to.

Epilogue

The house Sue and I built high on a hill in Littleton overlooks an artificial lake on the Connecticut River between New Hampshire and Vermont. To the west, five low mountain ranges climb deep into the Green Mountain State. To the far northern horizon, slivers of river wind toward what is called New Hampshire's Great North Woods, all under a generous expanse of sky. Truth be told, when I stand on my deck and watch an airliner miles overhead on the North Atlantic route, I feel a wistful tug and wish for a moment that I were up there in the captain's seat. But I fought that fight and lost. And in the years since my forced retirement I have found other battlefields, along with a measure of contentment.

Retirement was tough at first, and that old male Y chromosome thing still challenges me. Men have a tougher time leaving their jobs and professions because they link their identity to work. Women are forced to reinvent themselves throughout life. Many take their husband's name, dedicate years to child rearing and then sometimes return to careers they trained for decades before, or further their education to start anew. And statistically most will outlive their husbands. They deal with that better, too, having more friends than men do to provide support systems. Few men reach out like that. So perhaps Henry Higgins had it wrong; maybe the song from *My Fair Lady* should go, "Why can't a man be more like a woman?" Men might be happier and live longer.

It has been a broadening experience as I have pursued interests I never had time for when I was flying. Frankly, I approached this memoir with trepidation because I don't spend a lot of time thinking of the past. I look ahead. But writing it has been captivating and I think my story is worth telling. And I am still busy earning a living. When I left US Airways, a lump sum was available in lieu of a retirement annuity. I took the lump sum. After almost forty years in the plan, more than any other pilot with the company, it was a large amount of money, if not a fortune. Tragically, those who are receiving the annuity have had their benefit greatly reduced, some by two-thirds, because the company was shamefully allowed to terminate its retirement plan when it reorganized under Chapter 11 bankruptcy in 2002, dumping its obligation on the quasi government guarantor, the Pension Benefit Guarantee Corporation. It is yet another national scandal that corporations are allowed to use the bankruptcy process to stiff their employees by letting CEOs simply walk away from contracts on wages, health care, and pensions. I was lucky to get out when I did and consequently spend time managing our private portfolio, with professional help, from my well-equipped home office. Given the Bush depression, Sue and I have done as well as can be expected, but like many small investors we have lost a lot of asset value under George W. Bush that I don't expect to recover until there is a change in Washington.

I also serve on several volunteer boards and committees and I am a member of the Littleton Rotary Club. I am a delegate to the New Hampshire Democratic Party, serving as Chair of the North Country Democratic Committee and Vice Chair of the Grafton County Committee. I was proud to be an active member of former Vermont Governor Howard Dean's presidential campaign in northern New Hampshire and helped Senator John Kerry carry New Hampshire after he won the Democratic Party's nomination. While working and away from home half the time, I could never do these things.

And I am a writer. Although this memoir is my first book, I have written and published many papers, letters and opinion pieces over an activist's lifetime. I love to read and believe the written word is linked to the human potential. Conversely, I'm convinced that America's high rate of illiteracy is challenging our democracy.

Imagine life without a good book or newspaper and the small a world a person who can't functionally read or write inhabits. That is true poverty. Yet, according to the National Adult Literacy Survey, 21-23 percent of the adult population of the United States, or approximately 44 million people, scored at reading level 1, meaning they can read a little but not well enough to fill out an application, read a food label, or read a simple story to a child. Another 25-28 percent, or between 45 and 50 million people, scored at level 2. Literacy experts believe that adults with skills at levels 1 and 2 lack a sufficient foundation of basic skills to function in our society. How in the world is our country going to be competitive if a third of our adults can't read well enough to function?

How can our Democracy survive? Democracy is built on people having sound information upon which to vote. How can they get that information if they are not able to read a newspaper or a book? Radio, TV broadcasts and cable news aren't a substitute, particularly as the mega media corporations controlling them slip into fewer and fewer ultraconservative hands. Plus, Americans under forty tune the news out. Perhaps this explains why President Bush won a second term despite embroiling America in a senseless preemptive war in Iraq, which was based on faulty intelligence and lies, and despite tax policies that give advantages to the very rich, who don't need them, and an increase in the national debt of trillions of dollars. As this book goes to press in the middle of 2005, the ruling far right in America has little incentive to solve the illiteracy problem or create a renaissance for education. Their vision of American can only be achieved through fear and ignorance.

I have also had the time to run for the New Hampshire State Senate twice, in 2002 and again in 2004, losing but substantially narrowing the gap the second time in a strongly conservative district.

****

Since you now know most of the major events of my life, I can't close the story without answering the obvious question: Why did I, a reasonably sane and intelligent progressive, run for the Senate in one of the most politically conservative states in the country?

It is because I believe our country and my state, both of which I love, are in imminent danger from the politically far-right extremists now in control. Social and economic justice in America is being attacked at every turn by a well-financed far-right cabal with an outlook centered on fear and greed. Their vision is to turn back the clock to an idealized time when the "government" had little or no part in the welfare of people. The government existed exclusively for the benefit of big business—and most of all there were no income taxes to "soak the rich." It would be the time of President William McKinley on the cusp of the 20th century—before Teddy Roosevelt got in and started messing things up for big business.

Back then we didn't have expensive health care; we had essentially no health care. Senior citizens were no major problem because the life expectancy of a male at birth was only forty-six. Now it is almost seventy-four and seventy-nine for women. There weren't that many Americans to worry about, only 76 million compared to 281 million now. Rural America was dark and wouldn't be electrified until Franklin Roosevelt got into the White House and started blowing fuses on the corporate grid in 1933. Indoor toilets were a rich man's oddity; underwear was coarse and baths few and far between. But best of all to these modern mental midgets, there was no income tax; a libertarian U.S. Supreme Court had ruled it unconstitutional in 1895. The income tax wasn't reinstated until 1913 by the 16th Amendment to the Constitution. New Hampshire still doesn't have an income tax, or any other broad-based tax, making it the most regressive tax state in the country and a haven for the very rich.

President Bush and our far-right Congress (with the support of way too many Democrats) are making the hard choices, too, by giving massive tax cuts to the rich while running up the largest deficits in the history of the country. They will likely exceed $477 billion in 2004, $362 billion in 2005 and $2.4 trillion for the decade ending in 2013. During Bush's first administration, our markets lost trillions and unemployment was the highest since the Great Depression. But don't worry, the supply-siders say, the money will trickle down to the peasants. Historically, the only thing that has ever trickled down from such tax cuts smells foul.

While social programs and infrastructure are being sacrificed in the United States, our military budget is the largest in history, something on the order of $500 billion and climbing. At this writing, the war in Iraq alone was costing over a billion a week. We contribute only a billion a year to the United Nations and have been reluctant to pay even that. Must we protect ourselves and support our troops? Of course, but we shouldn't sacrifice our sons and daughters stupidly. As the world's only remaining superpower, the United States cannot squander its resources and power by being imperialistic, which in all of human history has never worked in the long run. Many veterans and patriotic citizens are scared stupid by the Bush administration's foreign policy; can you imagine how others in the world see it? To many, we are waging war against the world, making us a nation to fear and the object of their frustrations.

President Bush says repeatedly that the 9/11 attack on the World Trade Center was the defining moment of his administration. I believe him and the premise is frightening. Every day he, or Secretary of Defense Donald Rumsfeld, tells us we are at war. Hermann Göring, when asked how the Third Reich managed to get the German people to follow so blindly, said that it was "by making them feel they were in danger." Is the Bush administration using terrorism in the same way? After all, terrorism has existed throughout history. Islamic fundamentalists had attacked the World Trade Center previously with significant loss of life. For the United States to respond with paranoid fear is as self-destructive as instituting a police state in fear of crime. True, the United States is at war with Iraq. Following a dangerous policy of preemptive war, we invaded that country and, after overrunning it with a massive assault, claimed we had won and that the Iraqi people had been liberated. Their oil resources would be used to rebuild their country. The only trouble is that at the end of 2004 our troops were still dying there on an almost daily basis and the country was still in turmoil. Whom will we liberate next? Iran, Syria, North Korea? And, at the end of 2004, did anyone really think Afghanistan was much different than it was before the United States chased Al Qaeda and the Taliban into the hills? Osama bin Laden was still at large, Al Qaeda was again a mounting threat, the Taliban were regrouping, warlords controlled much of the countryside, and

10,000 U.S. and coalition troops were having trouble protecting an enclave in Kabul. The 2004 elections there did little to change that.

Beyond all that, I am troubled by the continuous far-right attacks on our system of government. It is not a conspiracy, which would be secretive. They come right out and tell us what they are doing. But that does not make it any less dangerous. The impeachment of President Clinton in the U.S. House of Representatives was a blatant attempt to remove a sitting president for political reasons. It compromised the effectiveness of Clinton's last two years in office and perhaps made us vulnerable to 9/11. Then a conservative U.S. Supreme Court foreclosed the election on Al Gore. Bush won five to four in the Supreme Court after Gore had won the popular vote. There was the successful recall ballot for Governor Gray Davis in California that was bankrolled by a millionaire Republican member of Congress and resulted in the election of the "terminator," Arnold Schwarzenegger.

The recall attempt was not for malfeasance but because the far right wanted another chance to oust him. Is that America?

Consider, too, the outrageous gerrymandering that the far right has successfully pushed in Texas and other states, which is threatening to take us back to the blackest days after the Civil War. And perhaps most threatening to our democracy is the vast amounts of money extremely wealthy people spend to buy elections. They say it is freedom of speech. The money is poured into mass TV assaults on our senses, while the media, controlled by the same financial interests, rakes in the money. Thirty second or one minute sound bites of little substance bombard an electorate, one-third of which are not functional readers. Is America now for sale?

My apologies for entertaining such serious issues at the close of what I hope has been something of a fun read. But this is an epilogue not an epitaph. My work is ongoing and our country needs us to be more than just spectators sitting on the sidelines. That's why I ran for the state Senate.

****

Shifting gears again, the hardest thing I find about growing older is that your family and friends seem to die around you—my Uncle

Ralph a couple of years before I retired, my close friend and skiing mentor, Ollie Cole, shortly after, Mother suddenly on Armistice Day, November 11, 1998. Had I continued flying I would have missed some wonderful days with her, so maybe the fates knew what was best after all. Sue's father died in April 1997, her mom in December 2000 after a long, incapacitating illness that left us both orphans—a term not often associated with people our age, but no less painful or true. Our dear friend and Mother's former nurse, Joyce Lasco, died in a tragic all-terrain vehicle accident; my ski buddy Mal Rosenthal succumbed to cancer. Near the other end of life's spectrum—and especially heartbreaking—was the death of my grandson Nicholas at the age of six months from congenital heart disease.

And there are others, but life goes on and, as many have often said, God doesn't give you more than you can handle. We've made some wonderful new friends, including journalists Tim McCarthy and Olivia Garfield. Tim, whom I acknowledged earlier, served as my campaign manager during my first Senate run. During our lengthy drives together on the campaign trail, we talked endlessly. Tim was always interested in my flying tales. He is the one who encouraged me to write my story and certainly the one who gave it a professional shine. But he is a good teacher and I am becoming a better writer.

As is the case with many families in modern day America, our children and grandchildren live busy lives hundreds of miles away and Sue and I needed more life around us. I had always wanted an Airedale terrier, the kind of dog Little Orphan Annie had. He was called Sandy in decades of cartoons and on Broadway. Our Belington terriers, Winston and Ditto, had lived long lives and were gone, as were Farley and Petunia, the two cats who completed our menagerie. Sue and I struck a deal and the search was on. Sue had always wanted a Red Abyssinian kitty. The Airedales would come from a wonderful breeder in western Ohio, Charlotte Autrey; the cats would be a brother and sister from a not- so-reputable breeder in central New Hampshire. The puppy we named Spencer, after Sir Winston Spencer Churchill, our dog Winston's namesake. Spencer's grandmother had actually played Sandy in the Broadway show. The following year we got his sister from the next litter and named her

Tracy. Spencer and Tracy just seemed a natural. The two kitties we named Zoie and Zack.

The two pups, now going on five and four years old, weigh eighty and sixty pounds respectively and fill our house with their loving, rollicking presence. I literally can't stop when walking from room to room without getting banged into. Unfortunately, Zoie came to us with a genetic defect that claimed her life after a few years and a valiant fight. Zack needed a buddy, which we found looking out from a newspaper ad and needing a home. He is a ten-year-old yellow tabby called Rudy. Zack immediately adopted him, but for a while the dogs thought he was sport to chase. But it is working out. Maybe some of those human problems I've been talking about will as well.

About the Author

Jerry Sorlucco was a commercial airline captain for nearly forty years, until federal regulations forced him to retire at age 60. From seat-of-the-pants flying to huge, computerized airliners, his career encompassed most of the history of commercial aviation in the 20th century. He began flying when he was 14. By age 18 he had his commercial pilot's license, although he was too young for any airline to hire him. He was a captain at 23.

Despite some near misses, Sorlucco ended his long career with no accidents and no major damage of any kind to the aircraft he commanded. That record earned him the reputation for being what pilots call "a good stick."

Sorlucco was a founder and vice president of the Professional Pilots Federation and an officer in the Airline Pilots Association. His flying career and professional activism, combined with an intense involvement in current and historical events, gave him the scope he needed to write A Good Stick.

Since his retirement, Sorlucco has run for the New Hampshire Senate twice and has become a leader in the state Democratic Party. He is at work on a new book titled *The Politics of Passion*. He lives with his wife Sue, two dogs and two cats in Littleton, New Hampshire.

Printed in the United States
37668LVS00006B/67-78

9 781420 848434